Mourning Unlived Lives

A Psychological Study of Childbearing Loss

JUDITH A. SAVAGE

CHIRON PUBLICATIONS
Wilmette, Illinois

The Chiron Monograph Series, Volume III

General Editors: Nathan Schwartz-Salant, Murray Stein
Managing Editor: Harriet Hudnut Halliday

Grateful acknowledgment is made to the following:

Begin & Garvey Publishers, Inc., for permission to reprint "Good-Bye Kim," by Peggi Barnicle, from *Ended Beginnings: Healing Childbearing Losses*.

Joseph Digman for permission to reprint "The Sitting Time," as originally published by Begin & Garvey Publishers, Inc.

Gael G. Jarrett for permission to reprint "The Baby Has Died," as originally published by the Cleveland Regional Perinatal Network in the newsletter *Feelings*.

Sherry L. M. Jimenez for permission to reprint "Stillborn," by the late Leonard Clark, from *The Other Side of Pregnancy*.

Candy McLaughlin for permission to reprint "Healing" from *Minnesota SIDS Newsletter*, vol. 4, no. 3 (Dec. 1983).

The C. V. Mosby Company for permission to reprint illustrations from *The Beginnings of Parent-Infant Attachment*, by Marshall Klaus and John Kennell.

Pantheon Books for permission to use specified excerpts from *Beyond Endurance: When a Child Dies*, by Ronald J. Knapp.

Princeton University Press for permission to quote in passim from volumes 5, 6, 7, 8, 9, 11, 12, and 18 of *The Collected Works of C. G. Jung*, trans. R. F. C. Hull, Bollingen Series XX.

Random House, Inc., for permission to reprint specified excerpts from "Requiem for a Friend" and "The Tenth Elegy," by Rainer Maria Rilke, from *The Selected Poetry of Rainer Maria Rilke*, ed. and trans. Stephen Mitchell.

Paul C. Rosenblatt for permission to reprint the bar graphs from *Bitter, Bitter Tears*.

Library of Congress Catalog Card Number: 88-10940
Printed in the United States of America
Book design by Elaine M. Hill

Library of Congress Cataloging-in-Publication Data

Savage, Judith A.
    Mourning unlived lives : a psychological study of childbearing loss
      p.   cm.
    Bibliography: p.
    Includes index.
    1. Bereavement—Psychological aspects. 2. Perinatal mortality—
Psychological aspects. 3. Parents—Psychology. 4. Archetype (Psychology).
5. Jung, C. G. (Carl Gustav), 1875-1961. I. Title.
    [DNLM: 1. Attitude to Death. 2. Bereavement. 3. Death—in infancy &
children. 4. Fetal Death. 5. Parents—psychology. BF 575.G7 S264m]
BF575.G7S28   1989
155.9'37—dc19
ISBN 0-933029-40-3 (pbk.)

88-10940
CIP

To my sons

A magic dwells in each beginning and,
protecting us, it tells us how to live.

Hermann Hesse

A categorical question is being put to [humankind], and [we are] under no obligation to answer it. To this end [we] ought to have a myth about death, for reason shows [us] nothing but the dark pit into which [we are] descending. Myth, however, can conjure up other images for [us], helpful and enriching pictures of life in the land of the dead. If [we] believe in them, or greet them with some measure of credence, [we are] being just as right or just as wrong as someone who does not believe in them. But while the [one] who despairs marches toward nothingness, the one who has placed . . . faith in the archetype follows the tracts of life and lives right into [one's own] death. Both, to be sure, remain in uncertainty, but the one lives against one's instincts, the other with them.

—C. G. Jung, *Memories, Dreams, Reflections*

Contents

Foreword

In the course of my childbearing years I had three children who died from miscarriage, stillbirth, and ectopic pregnancy, but ultimately I became the mother of two living sons.

When my son Brennan died just prior to his birth in 1981, I was devastated, confused, overwhelmed, lonely, isolated, and I certainly felt crazy.

I cried. I wailed. I felt guilty and looked for a cause. I sought out others who had been there. I remembered my son and tried desperately to keep him alive in my own life as well as in others'. On too many days I just wanted to give up, to go to sleep, and, yes, maybe even to die. And I searched for a perspective that would help me understand the meaning of my loss.

Little did I realize while I was in the middle of it that the human condition of pain, guilt, anger, and my questioning of my motherhood capabilities were all a natural part of the process of mourning, common to humans and mythological characters throughout time. I never found validation in the written word. Until now.

After I read *Mourning Unlived Lives*, a thoughtful and intense book, I understood even more why I had felt those feelings, behaved in those ways, and suffered as I had in my grief.

Judith Savage, a sensitive and understanding analyst, mother, and author, interprets such loss and showed me that the feelings I had were one and the same with all other mothers who have experienced the loss of a child. I benefited greatly from reading the case studies of her analysands. By understanding the universality of the problem, I could better understand the normalcy of my reaction and gain solace from this knowledge.

Mourning Unlived Lives presents a rare comparison and explanation of many popular bereavement models and examines their strengths and faults. Many parents and professionals fight for the right of bereaved families to love, remember, and deeply mourn their miscarried or short-lived infants' lives. I was interested to learn of the deep hold that Freudian psychology erroneously has on us: since he posited that the duration and intensity of grief depend on the length of the relationship, the all-too-widely held belief that these short-lived lives cannot be long mourned becomes more understandable, if ultimately wrong.

Judith presents a fresh perspective on this subject by sharing the psychology of Carl Jung. The Jungian perspective presents grief as a human experience with much uniformity in emotions and behavior, suggesting that such loss experiences are influenced by archetypal themes common to the experience of all humankind. The resolution of mourning requires that we understand the full extent of our loss and have its effect be made conscious.

Families need to make concrete their dreams, plans, and hopes for their baby by creating memories, seeing their baby, experiencing appropriate rituals and passages, such as a baptism and/or a blessing, a funeral and/or a memorial service. They need to act out their roles as parents to their child, to attach by saying hello before they are able to mourn and say good-bye.

Mourning Unlived Lives reviews the established work in the field of childbearing loss and interweaves it with practical and poignant prose and poetry. Through its case studies it provides new perspectives to most professionals by grounding much of childbearing loss and mourning in Jungian theory.

It is exciting to see how Judith uses dreams as an acceptable and almost necessary part of the integration process of loss. She offers many parents an opportunity to view their dreams, which they usually dread and fear, as something positive and helpful. Her interpretation and discussion of some specific dreams provide new insights into the field of childbearing bereavement from a practical and clinical perspective.

This book will be useful for parents to review some time after their loss. They will likely gain the perspective of how they fit into the realm of past and future, how they connect not only with Jesus' mother Mary but also with the gods and the goddesses of mythology as well as all parents past and present who have experienced the loss of their child. In addition, all care providers who want to better understand the emotions, behaviors, and process of mourning and integration after childbearing loss will benefit from reading this remarkable work.

The author offers a unique perspective based on sound principles, fresh interpretations, and a true empathy and understanding of the real people who suffer the heartache of the loss of their child.

Sherokee Ilse
Author of *Empty Arms: Coping with Miscarriage, Stillbirth and Infant Loss*

Introduction

Every human relationship ends. Moving to a new city, leaving home for the last time, divorce or death . . . every human relationship comes to an end. Grief is the expression of the loss of relationship, and the most common experience we all must face, over and over again. Throughout history we have created rituals that mark the passing of relationships, such rites of passage as marriage ceremonies, goodbye parties, funerals. We remember the good times and the bad; the funny and the sad; the embarrassing and the enriching. We remember the person, and our grief is not only for that person now gone, but for ourselves, left to find our way without him or her. The emptiness is profound; the loss is real. We say that a part of us died with that person's death, but seldom do we take that statement seriously.

In recent years we have begun anew to see the depth in human sorrow, to see its vitality and its significance. The subject of grief has become a popular topic in periodicals, books, motion pictures, and television. Deaths of parents, spouses, children, and close friends have been portrayed in these various media, expanding the spiritual as well as emotional and intellectual understanding of an experience none of us will ever be able to escape.

Any author, whether writing fiction or non-fiction, must find a standpoint or a voice for relating the information that is the subject of the work. When the narrator is involved with the story, the reader gets an entirely different slant on the plot and feels a kind of intimate connection that is otherwise missing in a narrative without a first-person voice. Although this book is non-fiction, the narrator's voice—my own—will be self-evident because of my personal experiences with grief. This book is the culmination of a decade-long enquiry that developed for the most part in the cluttered consulting room of Dr. Adolf Ammann in Zollikon, Switzerland. By the age of 33, I had not only lost my adoptive parents my natural parents, and my two brothers, but also an infant son. Given the multiplicity of my losses, I had to make my own meaning out of the experiences, and in the process I came upon psychological material that appeared to possess widespread application. And so I have chosen childbearing loss as my reference since it, like other losses, is an event that evokes sadness and disappointment. And yet, unlike other loss experiences, there is no "relationship," in the extrapsychic sense, to be mourned. It is for just this reason that I have chosen the topic, because it illustrates an aspect of human bereavement which has been, until now, unknown: the influence of the symbolic, archetypal image upon attachment and separation.

Childbearing losses are mourned not only for what was, but also for what might have been. A child developing in the womb possesses a physical reality of its own. But while it is still incubating, its personality remains unknown. And yet, a relationship exists as surely as if the child were being held in the parent's arms. At this early stage of attachment, the relationship is one in which the child is the object of the parents' imaginative projections. Then, if the wanted child dies, the parents grieve, of course. But also they mourn the child of the imagination, that part of themselves which seems now to have no possibility of embodiment in the world. Any true recovery must include the psychological retrieval of the contents of the imagination, which, with the child's death, have been feared to be lost. It is this aspect of the recovery that restores continuity of meaning to life. Apprehending the meaning of the symbolic losses, combined with the acceptance of the actual loss, strengthens the capacity to attach, eases the suffering of separations, and transforms bereavement into a spiritual journey that can strengthen the personality and deepen one's experience of life.

Any conceptualization of recovery from bereavement which includes this spiritual–symbolic dimension is difficult in a culture that devalues imagination and equates it, as the West does, with daydreaming and wishful fantasy. By valuing only what is concrete and materially visible, the already wide gulf between the sacred and the mundane is aggravated. In contrast, I want this book to focus on aspects of bereavement beyond the distressing symptoms (which is commonly regarded as the equivalent of recovery), to an apprehension of the uniquely personal meaning of the loss to the individual. Ironically, it is in the exploration of the deeper individual meaning of the loss that we encounter what is common to us all: the archetypal motifs that structure the human experience in the face of life's challenges.

Child-bearing losses have a pernicious effect upon the parents' self-images. Because of the heightened attachment inherent in pregnancy and the as-yet-unseparated physical condition between parent and child, there is a strong instinctive urge to protect and nurture the developing child. We feel a profoundly immediate experience of the life force operating in and because of us. When the pregnancy terminates prematurely with death for the child, the parents feel the corollary of the life force: they feel the negative, death-dealing aspect of nature itself. This can lead to a sense of personal failure, somatic guilt, rejection of the body, and an almost irresistible urge to self-destruct, predicated on the misguided desire to parent the deceased child, even in death.

From my experience, only by honoring the attachment and the genuine desire to parent are such agonizing effects thwarted. However, for the most part, our culture has denied the loss. The bodies of miscarried and stillborn children have been insensitively incinerated or disposed of in common graves. Family, friends, and others urge the bereaved parents to forget, get on with life and have other children. The parents' interest in the medical causes of the failed pregnancy have been treated as morbid preoccupation and have been dealt with by the medical community as if they were intrusive enquiries. The parents' yearning to hold their dead infant, the most natural of parental acts, has been viewed as macabre and unwholesome. Their desire to speak of their child and their inability to feel indifferent to its death even years later challenge our concepts of "healthy" recovery and cause the parents to be blamed for "refusing to let go." Yet, it is these very acts of holding, of talking, of loving, of attaching, all originating as they do in the instinctual realm of parenthood itself, that serve to inhibit the permanent derailment of psychic life which an identification with the dark side of nature provokes. It is through just these acts that good parenthood is manifested and lived out, psychologically strengthening the ego position, while at the same time mollifying the dreadful pull of the negative identifications.

Numerous self-help organizations have recently been developed to provide support and information to grieving parents. In addition, many books have been written that skillfully explain the medical, social and adjustment aspects of childbearing losses. The reader will find many of them listed in the bibliography. I have not wanted to replicate the work that has already been done. I am indebted to them for their scholarship, and for their kind efforts to ease the suffering of those finding themselves in such situations. But, given the nature of my losses and my own psychological interests, I have chosen to examine this topic from the perspective of depth psychology, to examine the intrapsychic, symbolic rule of the unconscious in bereavement. It is in the unconscious that attachments endure. By unraveling the mystery of the imaginative relationship, that is, the projections of the Self onto the unborn child, it becomes clear that primary relationships are not composed merely of interchangeable functional attributes and roles but are uniquely personal bonds that are generated from deep within and are as much a reflection of the individual soul as they are an accurate reflection of the other.

It is the nature of psyche to search, and many fortuitous events have assisted me over the years in my personal quest for meaning, in my own inner work, and in my work on this book as well. I am greatly indebted to those bereaved parents who have shared their dreams with me, as well as their sorrows and their hopes. Some have been my analysands, in which case I have changed their names. Others have responded to my solicitation for dreams as published in several perinatal loss newsletters. Others I have come to know and admire through the Pregnancy and Infant Loss Center, in Wayzata, Minnesota, most notably its founder, Sherokee Ilse, and board members, Susan Erling and Ronda Chin. They have been generous with their time and talent. I am also grateful to Florence Wiedemann for her guidance and support as well as for her advice in the early stages of writing this manuscript. I also want to thank Joseph Wakefield, Stan Marlan, and Murray Stein for their comments and contributions. My editor, Harriet Halliday, has been an artful and patient midwife to this present book. And, lastly, I wish to thank my husband, John Desteian, whose insight as a fellow analyst and whose confidence in the necessity of this work has supported me throughout its writing.

Chapter 1

When Nature Is Not a Mother

A ten week fetus is not pink jelly, but only the woman who loses her baby spontaneously is likely to know how human the tiny creature was and to grieve for it for the rest of her life.
—Germaine Greer, *Sex and Destiny*

Before I formed you in the womb I knew you. . . .
—*Jeremiah* 1:5

In our society we measure grief by the size of the coffin.
—Sherokee Ilse, author of *Empty Arms: Coping After Miscarriage, Stillbirth and Infant Death*

The Social Context of Perinatal and Reproductive Losses

Today is the day that I have been waiting for. I've been waiting nine months for this day to arrive. Now all I can do is remember this one time we had during those long nine months. This is the only memory we will ever have together. Being able to hold you, feel you in my arms, we created this one time together to last a lifetime.

The preceding quotation was shared with me by a young woman analysand who had entered therapy to understand why she remained depressed and unable to fully love her two surviving sons one year after the stillbirth death of her nearly full-term daughter. Her adjustment to the stillbirth of her only daughter was further complicated by the failure of her marriage. Although Sally and her husband had separated just prior to the birth of this third child, any hopes of reconciliation

1

were now complicated by their grief. Because of reproductive failure, both parents, each in their own way, now experienced themselves as less adequate. Their separate experiences of mourning further isolated them from each other. Where one partner needed to discuss the loss, the other tried to deny it. Within several months, Sally and her husband decided to divorce. Unconsciously influenced by their feelings associated with their childbearing loss, they felt that their marriage was unproductive and unable to nurture life. In the ensuing months, Sally was confronted with the multiple tasks of single parenting, coping with her grief for the lost child and the failure of her marriage.

After one year, her friends and family had grown impatient with Sally's grief. She, too, was impatient with herself, yet she felt unable to imagine a future that did not feel empty. Although she dearly loved her little boys, she felt strangely distant from them. She missed her daughter and had, as yet, not found answers to the incessant questions that nagged at her attention. Why? Why me? Why my little, helpless daughter? Where is the meaning in this?

Sally is just one of thousands of mourners—men, women, and surviving siblings—who have lost a child to the premature grips of death. Many have suffered the loss of older children—children who have been chronically ill, murdered, or killed in accidents; others have lost children at birth or just after birth (neonatal deaths); others have had children who were stillborn; others miscarried; others surrendered their children for adoption. All of these losses share a common tragedy: the uniquely grievous loss of a child. As Charles Garfield (1979, 316) states:

> It is to the parents of a (dead) child that fate delivers the severest blow. We fear for our children, as we fear for ourselves. Never have we lived or loved enough. Death always comes too soon.

Until very recently, reproductive losses were believed to rarely occur. However, as Panuthos and Romeo report (1984), they are suffered by many. "Over one-third of all babies conceived will not survive. One in every three women who conceives is touched by a childbearing loss. Over 195,000 parents lose their infants in stillbirth. Twelve to fifteen thousand infants succumb to Sudden Infant Death Syndrome (SIDS)" (xiv). Infant mortality rates listed in September 1986 ranked the United States at a poor seventeenth in the world

(*Minneapolis Star & Tribune*, Sept. 16, 1986). Despite our sophisticated medical technology, the United States currently has an 11.5 percent rate of infant mortality. The alarming failure to prevent infant mortality in America, despite the sophisticated medical technology available, finally reached national attention in 1988 when the Children's Defense Fund identified it as a national crisis and sought the immediate reform of the medical delivery system. According to the Children's Defense Fund report, low birth weight and prematurity together caused an overall increase in the infant mortality rate beginning in 1985. (Most noteworthy is the steady increase among minority populations.) Other childbearing losses, such as miscarriage or infertility, continue to be collectively disregarded. Cumulatively, these deaths become the "non-events" in the survivors' history (Lewis 1976). Statistics reveal only a percentage of their actual occurrence. For many women, miscarriages and abortions are not reported and are privately mourned.

Klaus and Kennell (1982) have reported that, until very recently, "everything involving a pregnancy loss was secreted and hidden. In the hospital, the staff quickly removed all evidence of the dead baby. The body was disposed of without funeral in a common grave. The whole episode was veiled in silence." With the advancing sophistication in medical technology, as Aries explains, "the nineteenth-century romantic model of death underwent a gradual evolution. It ended with the 'medicalization' of death, where everything in public life that reminded one of death became taboo. Death became indecent and mourning a malady" (Aries 1981, 583). This modern Western attitude, combined with the natural belief that children are not supposed to die, contributed to the collective denial of this very real sorrow.

Thousands of parents like Sally have privately struggled to comprehend the meaning of their loss. Current research has clearly described the etiological role of perinatal deaths (those occurring during pregnancy and delivery) and neonatal deaths (those occurring between birth and four weeks after birth) in the later development of psychiatric pathology and dysfunction. Culberg found, for example, that of 65 Swedish mothers who lost neonates, 19 had severe psychiatric disorders one to two years after the child's death (as quoted in Klaus and Kennell 1982, 173). Similarly, Kaplan's data revealed that of 45 families who suffered such a loss, three months later, 28 had severe marital problems that ended in separation or divorce. A total of 30 of these 45 families presented psychiatric difficulties in one or both of the spouses (Kaplan et al. 1973). Wolff found that nearly one-half of the women who had stillborn losses later refused to have any more children (1970). According to Knapp, "Child death is not only emotionally, psychologically, and physically the most painful experience one can encounter, it is also philosophically unintelligible; it defies the natural order of things" (1986, 14).

Models of Bereavement as They Apply
to Perinatal and Reproductive Losses

The experience of bereavement caused by a childbearing loss is shaped by many factors. The gender, age, and psychological and familial resources of the survivor are undoubtedly a crucial variable in determining its outcome. As Knapp (1986) outlines it, the circumstances of the death are also relevant. His study revealed discrete patterns of mourning among parents who lost a child following a long-term terminal illness, those who lost a child suddenly (including reproductive losses), and those whose children were murdered.

The progression of mourning is also dependent on the survivor's life experience with death and the quality of its resolution. Such life experiences are not confined to actual deaths of loved ones but also include other losses or "death equivalents," which Lifton describes as early "image-feelings of separation, disintegration, and stasis" (1983, 53).

The Jungian perspective is similar to the one described by Lifton inasmuch as past life experiences associated with the present loss are reconstellated and exert an influence on the current experience. These reconstellated contents form what Jung identified as a complex, which is composed of feelings, thoughts, memories, and imagistic residues of past experience organized in the unconscious around an archetypal core. According to Jung, complexes are essentially splinter psyches that have the capacity to "behave like independent beings" (Collected Works 8, par. 202, hereafter referred to as CW) and influence the behavior and perception of individuals despite their conscious efforts to the contrary.

The human experience of grief can be understood from a perspective of complexes and archetypal psychology on several counts. First, the uniformity of mourning, its typical emotions and behaviors and the evolution of these emotions through phases or patterns suggests that such personal experiences are influenced by archetypal themes common to the experience of mankind. Rosenblatt, Walsh, and Jackson (1976, 124) conclude from their cross-cultural analysis of 78 world cultures, for example, that "judging by the richness of our findings, . . . the nature of human interaction and long-term relations are such that, despite a wide range of differences among cultures, people around the world experience grief and commonly have the opportunity to express it." Such universality of experience is suggestive of an underlying predisposing patterning of human experience which Jung identified as the archetype. As Jacobi describes it:

> Archetypes are not inherited representations, but inherited possibilities of representation. They are channels, predispositions, river beds into which the water of life has dug deep. We must presume them to be the hidden organizers of representations; they are the "primordial pattern" underlying the invisible order of the unconscious psyche. (1959, 52)

In the second place, the archetypal influence on mourning also emphasizes the psychological necessity of comprehending the meaning of the loss. As Jung stated:

> The changes that befall humankind are not infinitely variable; they are variations of certain typical occurrences which are limited in number. When, therefore, a distressing situation arises, the corresponding archetype will be constellated in the unconscious. Since this archetype is numinous, i.e., possesses a specific energy, it will attract itself to the contents of consciousness. Its passing over into consciousness is felt as illumination, a revelation, or a "saving idea." (1956, par. 450)

The transformative experience of grief as described by many mourners includes an expansion of preexisting religious or spiritual ideas. Such experiences testify to a transformative element at work on the experience of loss which cannot solely be accounted for by the cessation of disturbing emotionality, confusion, or the effects of dispositional changes on the survivor.

Lastly, Jung's theory of the autonomous nature of the complex is descriptive of the actual experience of mourning. Similar to the behavioral effects of a constellated couplex, mourning has the capacity to overwhelm and dominate the conscious personality in such a way that mourners remain, at least for a time, unable to free themselves from its grip. The disturbing effects of mourning continue until the loss can be assimilated emotionally and result in a new distribution of psychic energy. The loss of the external object causes the mourner to suffer, not only over the loss of the loved one but also over the encounter with their own human fallibility, mortality, and the loss of self attributes believed to reside with the deceased.

The resolution of mourning demands that the full extent of the loss and its effects on the survivor be made conscious. As Jacobi states, "No complex can be resolved unless one faces the conflict that causes it, and this requires courage, strength, and an ego that is capable of suffering" (1959, 18).

Ultimately, each person grieves in his or her own idiosyncratic and personal way. However, general patterns do emerge and reveal a commonality in the usual mourning experience.

Since the 1950s, thanatological psychology has turned its attention to outlining the psychological process of bereavement. Bowlby, Parkes, Lindemann, Kübler-Ross, Marris, Raphael, and Kavanaugh, to name only a few, have established individual theories that described the discrete stages of psychological adaptation to a death. At this introductory juncture, I would like to briefly address their common findings so as to establish the phenomenological basis for my later discussions.

Most well known of the phase theorists is Kübler-Ross (1969). Through her research with terminally ill patients she developed a five-phase process of mourning as they considered their own imminent deaths: (1) denial; (2) depression; (3) anger; (4) bargaining; and (5) acceptance. Kavanaugh's model (1974), on the other hand, applies more directly to the experience of the survivor. He outlined seven stages: (1) shock and denial; (2) disorganization; (3) violent emotions; (4) guilt; (5) loss and loneliness; (6) relief; and (7) re-establishment.

Davidson (1979), studying 1200 bereaved adults who lost children, developed a four-dimensional process which he attributed to the earlier work conducted by Bowlby and Parkes. His phases included: (1) shock and numbness; (2) searching and yearning; (3) disorientation; and (4) reorganization. Lastly, Horowitz (1976) described a stress-response syndrome composed of four phases: (1) outcry-denial; (2) intrusion; (3) working through; and (4) completion.

Within each of these phase theories, the typical affectual responses of mourning are attributed to a category or phase. All forms of common grief symptomatology, such as "pangs of grief," depression, suicidal ideation, somatic distress, preoccupation with images of the deceased, auditory or visual hallucinations, labile moods, emotional isolation, anger, crying, are subsumed under the appropriate phases, thereby representing the natural progression of mourning. With regard to the loss of a child, many of these symptoms are exaggerated in intensity and the length of the bereavement process itself is often longer in duration. The unique factors complicating bereavement in infant and child loss are, as explained by Furman (1978), the incompatibility of the two simultaneously occurring psychological processes of detachment and attachment. Detachment, or the process of separation from the deceased, first begins through an identification by the survivor with the deceased person. Through identification, the mourner is able to retain attributes of the deceased which are then maintained as part of the mourner's own psychology. Psychologically, this identificatory process preserves the continuity of relationship between the survivors and the deceased. Later, when they are in a more stabilized ego position, the survivors are able to distinguish between those attributes belonging to themselves and those belonging to the deceased. The Jungian theoretical corollary of this process is that of projection, differentiation, and reintegration of the previously projected contents. From a Jungian perspective, however, this process involves a greater consciousness on the part of the survivor than is usually implied in the Freudian-based models. However, the act of psychological detachment assumes an external situation in which a sufficiently discrete personality of the deceased exists. This is not, however, the case in perinatal or neonatal death and is less operative in older child deaths as well. As Lewis describes it, "It is not possible for (adult) parents to take into themselves any part of a helpless newborn and make it adaptive." He argues that the mourning of an infant death is better understood as similar to the loss of a limb. The corresponding self-image of the parent is, in part, amputated by the death of the child, which then causes "others to shun [the mourner] as they would an amputee, for it fills them with fear and anxiety" (1978).

The unique factors inherent in miscarriages, stillbirths, and early-childhood deaths is the topic of this book. Through this work, I hope to expand the understanding of this unique loss by illustrating its archetypal patterning and the corresponding motifs that are activated at the time of death by the underlying archetypal parent-child paradigms that structure these relationships. Secondly, I intend to address the profound experience of meaninglessness, which is so dramatically constellated by a child death, with an examination of the individuation intent of the Self. The foundation of my subsequent comments, however, must first rest on the unique features of this type of mourning experience.

Knapp, in his recent book, *Beyond Endurance: When a Child Dies*, found six salient features common to parents who have lost children. These "common modal response patterns" of parents occurred in the vast majority of parents in his sample and were unique to this type of loss, either in kind or in intensity. As Knapp elaborates, "some of these common patterns carried a beneficial connotation . . . others were detrimental" (1986, 29). Regardless of their connotation, these modal response patterns represent natural aspects of the complex phenomenology of bereavement. The six common modal response patterns include: (1) the vow to never to forget the child; (2) the wish to die; (3) revitalization of religious beliefs; (4) a change of values; (5) more tolerance; and (6) shadow grief.

The Vow Never To Forget

Foremost among his findings is the need never to forget. Regardless of the age of the child or the circumstances of the death, the surviving parents felt compelled to remember the deceased child in a particularly intense way. They suffered most when those around them seemed to have forgotten the child. Intently, the parents clung to what memories they had, even if only a few, as in the case of a stillborn or neonatal death. As a consultant to a local Reach Out program for the Pregnancy and Infant Loss Center (in Wayzata, Minnesota), I was impressed by the loyalty of these parents to their deceased children. Photos, memories, memorial services, all were tender testimonies of their love for the deceased infant. I was deeply moved by the parent's genuine need to speak of the child, name it, hold its small body, arrange for memorial services. Often there were too few persons to share their memories with. As with Sally, relatives can grow impatient and want the bereaved to stop mourning. Yet, even a year later, Sally still felt unfinished with her grief and entered therapy in hope of completing it.

The vow to remember is often made in the poems of bereaved parents. These poems are as moving as the lamentful soliloquies of ancient grieving goddesses or the psalms worshipfully sung by Buddhist nuns. All grief springs from the same archetypal source. The following poems are but a few:

Good-bye Kim
I've carried you in my mind for five long years.
Haunting me.
Waking me at night in tears.
Asking why—no answer given.

Wanting to be with you,
yet
ties that hold me here not always stronger than you.

Living with the fear
   of having let you go too soon.
   But for whom was it too soon?

Learning that you won't be back.
   But knowing you are here
   in different things
     in wind,
     in light
     in faces of friends who care.

I'm finding you a place to stay
   that's soft and warm and safe.
A place where we can be together without hurt,
   without the tears and terror and screams.

It's in my heart, my firstborn child,
   this place where you can go.
Where we can visit
   and share the love we felt before.

So leave my mind and find my heart,
   where a welcome awaits your soul.
So we can dream of beautiful things,
   like flowers in the snow.

               —Peggi Barnicle (Panuthos and
                       Romeo 1984, 198)

The poem entitled "Stillborn" also reveals this commitment to remember.

Stillborn

I carried you in hope,
the long nine months of my term,
remembered that close hour when we made you,
often felt you kick and move
as slowly you grew within me,
wondered what you would look like
when your wet head emerged,
girl or boy, and at what glad moment
I should hear your birth cry,
and I welcoming you
with all you needed of warmth and food;
we had a home waiting for you.

After my strong labourings,
sweat cold on my limbs,
my small cries merging with the summer air,
you came. You did not cry.
You did not breathe.
We had not expected this;
It seems your birth had no meaning,
or had you rejected us?
They will say that you did not live,
register you as stillborn

But you lived for me all that time
in the dark chamber of my womb;
and when I think of you now,
perfect in your little death,
I know that for me you are born still;
I shall carry you with me forever,
my child, you were always mine,
you are mine now.

Death and life are the same mysteries.

—Leonard Clark (Jimenez 1982, xi)

Knapp interprets the vow to never forget as "a means to deal with the emptiness of the future . . . by filling this void with the images of the child they once had, through thoughts, memories, and open discussion. Only in this way does loss become a reality" (1986, 31). Thus, Knapp emphasizes the adaptive function of remembering. As such, the parents are compelled to eventually face their loss and overcome the tragedy that has threatened their personal survival. Knapp's emphasis on the reality function aspects of grief is typical of the theoretical perspective of most modern psychologies. No doubt adaptation to the reality of death is essential to recovery. However, while remaining exclusively concerned with ego–adjustment criteria, the transformative and spiritual dimensions of mourning are inadequately comprehended. To this end, the vow to remember serves to preserve the reality of the intra-psychic relationship between parent and child until the loss can be integrated, the psychic economy restored, and the meaning of the loss apprehended. The outcome of the mourning process does not simply return us to the same place we were before the child's death; rather it changes us, and it is the nature and scope of the change that must be made conscious. Similarly, Jung, von Franz, Hillman, Langer, and Lifton argue that depth psychology can and should return us to the task of elucidating the "experiential transcendence" inherent within the "sense of continuing between life and death" (Lifton 1983, 34). Cumulatively, this perspective emphasizes a symbolic or archetypal approach. Although also concerned with reality function, the symbolic approach is additionally concerned with the inherent transformative potential of mourning. As such it is more able to comprehend the crisis of "meaning" which is activated by the death of a loved one.

As stated by Lionel Corbett in his unpublished manuscript, "Suffering and Incarnation," "when the ego truly understands the meaning of its suffering, the process of incarnation is complete." By incarnation, Corbett is referring to the eventual integration or embodiment of a transpersonal experience of the Self as manifested by the constellation of archetypal imagery and themes. He adds, "Because of the imago-dei aspects of the Self . . . the archetypal manifestations of the divine [lead] to either spiritual or psychological growth" (Corbett 1986).

Throughout this work I will attempt to illustrate the efficacy of an archetypal perspective which responds more fully to the breadth and depth of the experience of mourning as a whole. Modern ego psychology, based on a Freudian drive model, in my opinion, inadequately explains the unique phenomenology of mourning over childbearing loss. The death of a child, more than any other grief, illustrates the deficiencies of this model.

Returning to Knapp's first finding, the prevalence of the parental "vow to remember" serves two psychological ends. Although undoubtedly furthering the conscious adaptation to the death, it more importantly maintains the intercontinuity of the parent–child relationship aimed toward a potentially transformative end, which is directed by the central archetype of the personality, the Self.

As Jung described it, "The self is not only the centre but also the whole circumference which embraces both conscious and unconscious, it is the centre of this totality, just as the ego is the centre of the conscious mind" (1953, par. 444). From this statement it is clear that intense experiences such as mourning would engage not only the conscious personality but also activate unconscious contents. Thus, survivors dream of the deceased, experience quasi-hallucination of the deceased's presence, and past experiences of loss are reactivated and add to the intensity of the present bereavement. Overall, the psychic economy as a whole is disturbed. Adaptation to the external reality of bereavement would therefore demand more than a mere change in habits and a return to functioning. To this end, the continuity of the parent-child bond is psychologically preserved so that such intra-psychic adaptations can be realized.

In the circumstances of infant bereavement, the parent's identity as an effective, nurturing parent has been thwarted. As mortal parents who were unable to prevent the child's suffering and death, whose love was experienced as not enough, these parents are then psychologically vulnerable to an ego-identification with the devouring Terrible Mother or Negative Father archetype.

Such identifications account for the intensity of guilt experienced by parents who have suffered reproductive losses. As Palinski and Pizer (1980, 126) write: "Undoubtedly the strongest emotional response after a miscarriage is guilt. Without exception, every woman we talked with had experienced or was still experiencing feelings of guilt. They looked back for months seeking a probable cause in their own behavior just prior to the miscarriage." This same prevasive sense of guilt was also expressed by my analysand Sally. In her journal account of the still-birth, entitled "Silent Baby Sister," she writes,

> *My mind will not let me rest about your death. What have I done wrong, how could I have prevented you from dying? I have such a tremendous sense of guilt. I've cooped myself up in the house for fear that something else will happen. Here in my house no one can hurt me. Only the memories that I am left with. Oh, God, please, I hope you know what you are doing because it is very unclear to me.*

Just as a parent can become identified with an archetype such as the negative parent, so is the defenseless infant likely to be perceived in association with the positive aspect of the "divine child" archetype. This association can initially complicate the mourner's ability to sep-arate from the child's "image." It may also diminish the capacity to express love toward any surviving children who, at least temporarily, are unconsciously compared against the "divine" image associated with the dead child. As with Sally, her daughter represented a lost aspect of herself that, in contrast to her two sons, offered her the possibility of experiencing something profoundly different as a parent. Despite her love for her sons, the image of this lost daughter became synonymous with Sally's own unfulfillment. Not having a daughter, she feared that her maternity and her womanhood was lessened. For a time she viewed her sons in stereotypic ways. She felt they needed her less as young men. As boys they were more independent and their need for security and nurturence was experienced as only demands for attention. To Sally, the child needing her maternal attention was her deceased infant daughter, who symbolically corresponded with her own vulnerable and lost feminine self.

In a later stage of devlopment within the mourning process the association of the dead child to the Divine Child archetype does not result in an inflationary view of the child but in a separation between the actual child from its corresponding divine image. This differentiation between "image" and child enables the real loss to be accepted as permanent; the Divine Child image can then act as an inner figure, a guide or psychopomp to the individuation process within the grieving parent.

The constellation of such impersonal contents from the collective unconscious exerts a "bigger-than-life" influence upon a person. These archetypal forces, however, are not within the realm of personal responsibility. As Eisendrath-Young explains,

> *The negative mother complex is organized around the archetype of the "Terrible Mother." This complex expresses the instinctual-emotional responses to the negative aspects of nurturing or attachment. Incorporation, suffocation, stagnation [and certainly death], define her character. When the complex is attributed to a woman, or when a woman feels identified with the complex, she experiences herself as having more power than she rationally knows she has. She condemns herself for flaws which are exaggerated and beyond the responsibility of human beings.* (1984, 31)

A similar process occurs for the father of a childbearing loss. Identified with the impersonal, negative aspect of the masculine archetype, he may feel he has failed his offspring through defective fertilization or his inability to exert sufficiently heroic actions and rescue the child from the jaws of death. As the experience of these parents clearly attests, the death of the child activates these archetypal motifs and the surviving parents then feel that they are, in some irrational way, at fault for the child's death.

Furthermore, because of the child's death, these parents are then denied the opportunity to manifest a nurturing parenthood which, in a compensatory fashion, would extricate them from their identification with the negative aspects of this complex. It is only through the act of affectionate and fond remembering that they are able to express symbolically their loving parenthood. Thus, the vow to remember is, at its most important level, the means through which the parents can both "incarnate" the child, thereby making him an *object* of their love, and realize their own parenthood. The alternative would be to remain, at least in part, identified with the archetypal death-parent, which no doubt contributes to the unwillingness of some parents to have other children.

A second psychological alternative is the use of the psychological defense of detachment. As Bowlby's work indicates, when children are faced with no effective means to resolve their grief, their primary defense mechanism is detachment. According to Bowlby, the tripartite process of mourning (protest, despair, and detachment) observable in children is an instinctual and evolutional defense designed to preserve the species. Adults, however, have greater psychological resources than do dependent children. Most notably, adults possess a more refined ability to "make corresponding changes in the internal, representational world, and to reorganize, and perhaps reorient, one's attachment behavior accordingly" (Bowlby 1980, 18). Nonetheless, a detachment defense is observed in such indications of incomplete mourning as the protracted use of denial, or what Mitscherlich described as the inability to mourn.

Knapp discovered that the "vow to remember" occurred in nearly all parent couples in his study. This is also consistent with other research. Although its intensity was diminished with time, it remained a life-long vow which did not, however, prohibit a satisfactory adjustment or resolution to the mourning. Rather, it seemed to strengthen it. The vow not to forget the deceased is, of course, most prevalent among relationships characterized by strong attachment and proximity to the survivor and represents a fairly common and normal response to such losses. Lindemann (1944), for example, found a similar phenomenon in his study of mourners, where he discovered that a significant number of survivors reported a preoccupation with images of the deceased, including both auditory and visual hallucinations. Similarly, Parkes, in his well-known study of London widows, discovered four discrete processes operative in normal mourning, the last two of which are relevant here. A significant number of those who had resolved their grief "maintained a belief that the loss was not permanent and that reunion was possible." This "resulted in the recognition that the loss had in fact occurred, *combined* with a feeling that links with the dead nonetheless persist, manifested often in a comforting sense of the continuing presence of the lost person" (Bowlby 1980, 140).

However, the intense emotional attachment that exists between parent and child, a relationship which is characterized by the heightened expectation of the parent to protect and nurture the vulnerable infant, makes the vow to remember a more likely occurrence in this kind of bereavement.

Lifton, in his recent book, *The Broken Connection: On Death and the Continuity of Life*, argues for a psychology "evolutionary in spirit and genuinely biological in its focus on image making." He states that it is through our inherent human capacity to imagine that we remain "symbolically connected to immortality" (1983, 55). He later concludes that "the survivors' psychological needs include *both* connection and separation from the deceased" (*ibid.*, 96).

Modern collective mentality, however, denies this natural need to remain emotionally connected to the deceased, characterizing it as non-adaptive. The cultural and psychological factors contributing to this condition will be elaborated in subsequent parts of this manuscript. The first finding of Knapp, however, clearly indicates that the "vow to remember" has a vital role in restoring the psychological equilibrium of the mourner and contributes to a later transformative expansion of the conscious personality of the bereaved.

The Wish To Die

The second finding of Knapp's study is the high frequency of the parents' "wish to die." It is a well-known fact that grief is a traumatic experience, but less well understood is the intensity of the grief of parents who have lost a child. Our cultural perspective has been shaped by, among other factors, Freud's primary role in the evolution of modern psychology. Freud's early work, *Mourning and Melancholia*, written in 1917, is a cornerstone for subsequent thought regarding the psychology of grief. Predicated on the primacy of drives and their derivatives, the mental economics of Freud's libido theory described mourning as the eventual decathexis of all libido from the attachment to its object. The normal outcome of this energetic process is an acceptance of the reality of the death. He adds: "Each single one of the memories and hopes which bound the libido to the object is brought up and hyper-cathected, and the detachment of the libido from it is accomplished" (Freud 1963, 166).

In this quantitative framework, achieving resolution of the mourning is directly related to the length of the relationship with the deceased. More simply stated, the more numerous the memories and the lengthier the attachment history, the longer the process of decathexis. However, contrary to this assumption, infant death often precipitates a more intense and longer lasting grief than that of other losses. The high percentage of persons who suffer acute periods of wishing to die illustrates the inadequacy of such an equation. These parents have few, if any, concrete memories from which to decathect. As with reproductive and neonatal losses, they may never have seen or held the child. None-theless, the intensity of their grief threatens to shred the fabric of their lives. Desperately seeking to remain psychologically connected to their deceased child, suicide offers them the distorted hope of being reunited in death. Thoughts of suicide are common to many survivors of other types of losses; however, the survivors of a deceased child remain in greater jeopardy. The occurrence of the acute wish to die and the inten-sity of mourning remained enigmatic to Freud. He acknowledged: "Why this process of carrying out the behest of reality, bit by bit, which is the nature of a compromise, should be so extraordinarily painful is not at all easy to explain in terms of mental economics" (Freud 1963, 166). It can, however, be understood from an archetypal perspective.

Grief for the loss of a child has frequently been enacted within the mythical and religious realm. Inanna, the Sumerian goddess from the third millennium B.C., for example, laments the passage of Dumuzi, her son/lover, to the underworld:

> Into his face she stares,
> seeing what she has lost.
> His mother who has lost him
> to death's kingdom.
> Oh, the agony she bears,
> shuddering in the wilderness,
> she is the mother suffering so.
> (Sanders 1971, 163)

The legend of the creation of the Buddhist Order of Nuns (*Bhik-kunis*), found in the Tenth Khandhaka, relates how Mahāprajāpatī, the aunt who nursed the Buddha after his mother Mahāmāyā's death, is joined by 500 followers, all bereaved mothers. In the legend, Mahāpra-jāpatī, also called Gautami, walks 120 miles barefoot and sorrowfully weeping to seek the consolation of the Buddha. Her fellow sisters, all grieving for their lost children, wail psalms of their remorse. Vasetthi, who later became a nun, cries:

> Grief struck for my son
> mad-minded, out of my senses,
> I was naked,
> with wild hair
> I wandered anywhere.
> I lived on trash heaps,
> in a graveyard,

and by the light of highways,
three years wandering
starved and thirsty.
     (Rhys-Davies 1932, Cantos VI and L)

And, lastly, the suffering of the Christian Virgin Mary is dramatically described in this fifteenth-century lyric:

Her hair, her face, she all to-rent,
She tugged and tore with great torment,
She brake her skin both body and breast,
And said these words as ever she went:
"Filius regis mortuus est."
     (Brown 1930, 9)

These psalms and verses illustrate what Esther Harding discussed in her chapter on maternity in *The Way of All Women*. There she states:

In many women, love of the offspring remains an almost animal like quality, which cannot be called love of the child, of the person at all. The child represents to the mother a little piece of herself which has become partly separated and which she passionately loves on account of the still unbroken bond with herself. (1970, 179)

Harding adds that the need for differentiation between the child and mother is crucial to the resolution of grief. It is accomplished "*with the mother's release from identification with the good-bad maternal instinct. It can only take place through a psychological differentiation of herself from her child,* by which she grants them the right to live their own lives and die their own deaths—to suffer as well as enjoy" (1970, 187; emphasis added).

As Harding elaborates, "To understand the experience of maternity it is necessary to inquire into the nature of maternal feeling . . . The desire for the conservation of life, and that at all costs, is the outstanding characteristic of mother love. She *must* conserve it" (1970, 178). Parents who have lost a child to death cannot help but feel that they have failed in their enactment of the instinctual and human act of procreation and the perpetuity of their personal heritage. In infant losses, before the possibility is realized to adequately differentiate from the child "object," the bond between the parents and the child is best understood as a *participation mystique*, an unconscious identification between subject and object. Therefore, with the untimely death, the parents cannot easily

separate from the deceased child, and their identification with it becomes regressive in character. More simply stated, their personal lives
are felt to be meaningless, and they experience a "loss of soul." Suicide
expresses their hopelessness, and, by sacrificing their own life, they
hope to reunite with the lost child, protecting it in death. Through the
enactment of this self-sacrifice, the parent attempts to symbolically
realize a "good-parent" identity; all-loving and self-sacrificing toward
the good of the child.

This struggle is echoed in the following comments by parents, as
quoted in Knapp:

> *I had no reason to live. I didn't really want to live. I think about it often
> . . . how easy it would be to simply "lose control" of the car while
> driving.*

> *I stared at the gun for the longest time! It would have been so easy. I was
> ready for it. Yes, I wanted to die. I wanted to be with Billy again. I
> thought if I died I would be able to see him and touch him again. I
> couldn't think of anything else for weeks.* (Knapp 1986, 33)

Revitalization of Religious Orientation

This painful struggle with one's own desire to live contributed to
Knapp's third finding, a high incidence in the change of the survivor's
religious orientation in a positive direction. Over 70 percent reported a
renewed or intensified belief in a spiritual dimension. For many, this
was expressed within an organized or pre-existing faith. For others, it
was a less-structured belief in a "greater power." For nearly all, it took
the form of "rekindling a belief in some sort of reunification with the
child after the parent's own death" (Knapp 1986, 35). Thus, a significant number of parents reported that they were no longer afraid of
death itself and eventually were more able to relish life and its offerings.
Through the painful journey of mourning they felt themselves to have
changed.

For many parents, with preexisting religious beliefs, their journey
into the underworld of mourning began with a desperate search to
understand the meaning of their loss. Personal struggles with their own
mortality and its limitations, with their profound depression, their
isolation, the injustice they felt over their child's death—all these tore
at their belief in a merciful God. For others who lacked a preexisting
religious orientation, the question of meaning was nonetheless compel-

ling. The evocation of a spiritual quest in the face of death is common in history. As Neumann states, "Through the experience of death, man enters the realm of the powers which otherwise he touches only fleetingly in especially elevated moments of experience." Neumann says we encounter "a familiarity with the transpersonal realm which unites life and death" (1976, 12). With the knowledge of this transpersonal element, the individual then experiences change. The form of this change may be the renewal of a preexisting religious belief or an idiosyncratic spirituality unique to the individual. Regardless, each parent had wrestled with the loss and for some "the numinous was experienced as part of his moment of fate, his Kairos" (ibid., 15). At times of crisis, such as the loss of a child, our conscious orientation is threatened. As Jung states:

> *The collapse of the conscious attitude is no small matter. It always feels like the end of the world, as though everything had tumbled back into original chaos. One feels delivered up, disoriented, like a rudderless ship that is abandoned to the moods of the elements. So, at least, it seems. In reality, however, one has fallen back upon the collective unconscious, which now takes over the leadership.* (1966, par. 254)

Jung elaborates: "But once the unconscious contents break through into consciousness, filling it with its uncanny power of conviction, the question arises of how the individual will react" (ibid.). He outlines three possibilities: (1) a regressive restoration of the persona; (2) inflation caused by an unconscious identification with the Self; and (3) transformation.

A regressive restoration of the persona is seen in the many behaviors of unresolved mourning, such as mummification—an unwillingness ever to change the child's room or to release his or her belongings. It is also present in too quick a desire to have another child (mislocation). Central to this defense is the belief that one cannot endure the loss or imagine a future without the dead child present. Adaptation is prohibited by the maintenance of a provisional life-style, a regressive turning back to "a measure one feels one can fill" (Jung 1966, par. 259). The grieved parent attempts to hold still the passage of time. This is, psychologically, a period of waiting, or stasis. The parent, most often the mother, awaits the child's return. Although this is a transitory phase in normal bereavement, it can evolve into a fixed defense against the pain of the loss. It is characterized by an idealized valuation of both the lost child and parenthood. No doubt it serves a compensatory purpose as an unconscious attempt to expiate feelings of guilt and failure. However, the personal self-sacrificing of one's own life to the delusion that the child may return prevents the survivor from realistically facing his or her fears of guilt and thus being free from its dominance.

An inflationary identification with the Self is observed among those parents whose grief remained inconsolable. As Jung states, "they are seized by a sort of pathos, everything seems pregnant with meaning, and all effective criticism is checked" (1966, par. 262). Unconsciously, they may regard their grief as more profound than that of others, holding themselves up as martyred "prophets" or experts on sorrow. Such an identification with the Self can also be negatively inflated. The mourner may remain consumed by grief, unable to turn attention to the matters of life, a psychological condition similar to Klein's concept of a depressive position in which the developing child is unable to integrate the ambivalent aspects of the good/bad mother and consequently negatively inflates his or her own badness. Ultimately perceiving themselves as powerless, the mourners remain unable to reconcile the ambivalent aspects of their parental Self images. Furthermore, as Jung explains, persons caught in this defense "may purposely expose themselves to the dangers of being devoured" (ibid., par. 261). As such, they unconsciously become identified with the archetype of the sacrificial victim. This dynamic is observed behaviorally, for example, in the unrestrained use of chemicals as an anesthetic to emotional pain. As the drug or alcohol intoxicates and romanticizes the sorrow, the user loses his personal identity by its continued use.

Psychodynamically, this is a condition of the ego's identification with the Divine Victim aspect of the archetypal shadow. In this condition, the bipolar dimensions of the Self are split. According to Tristan Cornes (1985), the Divine Victim is a negative, inflationary identification with the Self. Restitution within the ego–Self axis requires the acceptance of the "sad truth," that the good and the bad are necessary attributes of the whole (ibid., 220). This results from a psychological shift from an identification with the Divine Victim to that of personal victim who accepts only mortal responsibility for his or her failures or guilt.

Maintaining an identification with the Divine Victim archetype ultimately weakens the adaptive resources of the individual, which may culminate in suicide or chronic depression. It is in recognition of the powerful pull of archetypal death imagery that cultures have established rituals and forms of behavior for the mourner. In this way, the collective helps to sever too close an identification with the collective unconscious.

The transformative outcome of grief comes only with great sacrifice. It takes place, in the words of Neumann, "by way of initiation which leads through a dangerous labyrinth pregnant with death, and in which no conscious orientation is possible" (1976, 8). With the loss of a child, the parent survivor experiences a personal loss of soul. This loss of soul occurs with the death of the child who, not only loved for its own sake, is also the carrier of unconscious parental projections. Such projections are fundamental to the natural process of human attachment. As Jung described it, active projection is the psychological process of creating "magical ties between people." It is a fundamental process of bonding and necessary for later development of empathy. This process of attachment is described by Jung as follows:

In order to establish relationship, the subject detaches a content—a feeling for instance—from himself, lodges it in the subject, thereby animating it, and in this way draws the object into the sphere of the subject. (1971, par. 784)

With the child's death, these unconscious parental projections onto the child, which originate from the first awareness of conception, cannot incarnate or manifest themselves within the realm of the external, conscious sphere. Thus, the archetypal intent is thwarted. Those aspects of oneself that are projected onto the wished-for child, such as a sense of future and immortality, or one's hopes and wishes for the child's life, are, with the child's death, feared permanently lost. Thus, one feels profoundly diminished, as amplified by the etymological meaning of the word bereavement, stemming as it does from the same root as "to rob"—hopes literally have been stolen away.

As illustrated by the situation of my analysand Sally and her husband, their fragile marriage could not withstand their pronounced feelings of inadequacy constellated by their daughter's death. Their inability to give birth to a healthy and normal child was unconsciously perceived as synonymous with their inability to nurture each other within the marriage. The dead child was symbolically associated with other experiences within the relationship, namely, a feeling of "deadness" in their affections for each other, which added to their dissatisfaction with each other. Although they had hoped to have a future together, a belief which prompted them to accept this last pregnancy, that future was now experienced as ended with the death of the child.

The natural process of psychological projection does not, however, cease without cause. As Jung states, "it does so only when the need arises, when the absence of the projected contents is a hindrance to adaptation and its withdrawal into the subject has become desirable" (1971, par. 783). With the death, mourners must then become conscious of the nature of their projections and, through a differentiation between Self and other, re-embody the lost "soul" within themselves.

The loss of soul is also experienced by the survivors as a loss of personal ego identity. If overwhelmed by an unconscious identification with the impersonal numinosity of the parental archetypes, the conscious personality becomes less distinct. Ego identification with, for example, the negative aspect of the Terrible Mother archetype, can cause a parent to feel genuinely responsible for the child's death. Although searching for cause is common to childbearing loss, the inability to nurture and protect the infant makes an identification with the negative aspect of the archetypal parent more likely. Furthermore, the intensity of grief predisposes the grieving parent to a weakened ego state, which enhances the possibility of being overwhelmed by unconscious contents. If such a condition is also combined with a prexisting tendency for self-recrimination and blame, the bereaved parent may be unable to ward off such negative identification without heroic effort. Under the domination of a negative identification, a mother may feel unable to express her positive maternal qualities to her surviving children, as was the case for my analysand Sally.

Central to Jungian psychology is the primacy of the Self as the architect of the total personality. Attributed to the Self is an intent to make itself manifest, or incarnated, within the conscious personality. Unlike all other pyschologies, which assume the ego to be the primary nucleus of the personality, Jung described the relationship between ego and Self, also called the ego-Self axis, in the following way: "The ego stands to the Self as the moved to the mover, or as object to subject, because the determining factors which radiate out from the Self surround the ego on all sides and are therefore supraordinate to it" (1969c, par. 391).

The self-regulating nature of the psyche is evoked through the activation of the transcendent function. Experienced as symbol, whether in dreams, visions, affects, or synchronistic events, the transcendent function arises from the tension of opposites and the struggle of restoring meaning to one's life.

Combined with the conscious cooperation of the ego, it can produce a healing outcome. As Neumann described it, "consciousness originated when, out of the unconscious tension of the archetypally directed situation, the lightning of illumination and revelation flashes for the first time" (1976, 10). Although referring here to the evolution of consciousness in the species of man, this process is nonetheless an analogue for the operation of the transcendent function within the individual psyche. It is this personal experience of the numinous that later revitalized the spiritual beliefs among the parents of Knapp's study. Similar experiences were also reported by Panuthos and Romeo (1984) as illustrated by the following examples:

> *I ache to know, to understand. I hope to set out all my questions that I may come to find acceptance. My faith is trying to grow, and so I will loosen the seams, let down the hems, and fashion a new garment. I may need to work and rework it before it fits.*

> *I am willing now for God to be God—not a spirit made to my own image, but a spirit unto Himself.*

In the course of researching this work, I received numerous correspondences from mothers who responded to my request for dreams as published in several infant-loss newsletters. Many described their acceptance of their child's death as first echoed in their dreams. This is dramatically illustrated by two dreams sent to me by a woman whose infant son died at birth due to a prolapsed umbilical cord. The first dream occurred one week before delivery and unconsciously prepared her for the baby's death, a fact that she did not know of at the time of the dream.

> *I am standing at the bottom of a large hill that is covered with ice. At the side of the hill stood a person holding a tiny bundle in his arms. I knew the bundle was my baby, and the being that held him was a very gentle, loving "entity." I tried to follow them up the ice hill, but I kept sliding down. At the top of the hill was a thin red line that stretched across the sky. The sky was pitch black. The only word spoken was "Sunday."*

The prophetic nature of this dream is deeply impressive. The "entity" is a spirit form, like the angel of death itself. He holds her tiny son "gently" but the dream ego is unable to make it up the "icy" hill and join them. The ice is symbolic of the "coldness" of death and the experience of separation. On the horizon, heaven and earth are separated by a "thin, red line" which symbolizes the impenetrable boundary between life and death that later, tragically, separated this mother from her son. Most remarkable is the last line, "the only word spoken was the word 'Sunday.'" Her son died the following Sunday.

This same mother also reported a second dream, which occurred on the day of her son's funeral. She dreamed:

The "being" I saw in my earlier dream appeared again with the bundle in his arms. He gently unwrapped the bundle and it was my son. He was pink and perfectly radiant. It was very comforting. He was dressed in a gown and bonnet, beautifully trimmed in Chantilly lace.

The mother added in her letter: "I had not seen my baby nor did I have any knowledge of what he had been buried in. I later learned that he was, in fact, buried in a christening gown trimmed with Chantilly lace, chosen by his grandmother." She concluded, "My knowledge of the detailed lace is something that I cannot pass off as a mere coincidence."

Carol, a mother who lost her six-week-old daughter Jenna to Sudden Infant Death Syndrome provided me with another dream that also seemed to presage the death. Carol was impressed by the fact that in the dream, the sex of her unborn child was revealed and that the child's grandfather, who had died 10 months before Jenna, is seen holding the baby.

I am in the delivery room. I have had the baby. I asked the doctor the sex of the child and there was no response. Then, suddenly my father was standing there holding the newborn. He was smiling, he said "It's a girl." Then he started crying. (It seemed odd.) In the dream I wanted to get a picture of my Dad and the baby but I realized you can't take pictures of ghosts.

Carol reported that her father did not appear to be crying for joy at the birth of the granddaughter but rather as if he knew something Carol herself did not. After Jenna's death, Carol dreamed again of her father in the company of her daughter. In this dream, she saw her father and Jenna in white gowns in a foggy place. She adds, "I remember that Jenna was standing next to Dad and he was holding her hand and they seemed very happy!" Since Carol was very close to her father, whom she regarded as a loving and understanding parent, she felt comforted by this last dream. Psychologically, the image of her child in the protective custody of her father helped free Carol from the common fear that the deceased child's soul remains isolated and unprotected in some other liminal space or period of time. This same idea is observed in the Catholic conception of limbo as well as in many other religious concepts regarding transitional phases between death and the assumption of the soul or spirit into a higher realm. On the personal level, however, the dream reassured Carol that her daughter was cared for by her grandfather-spirit-guardian and thereby helped to free Carol from her persistent worry that she had abandoned the child to death.

Similarly, an analysand of mine whose daughter was stillborn, dreamed one-and-a-half years later:

My baby girl is nestled in a great warm nest. There are many other nests, each with babies, within this cave. It is safe and warm there and she is a happy baby.

This dream provided her with a comforting image of her much-wanted daughter nestled in the bosom of the Great Mother. After the dream, she felt more able to accept the loss while still believing in some form of nurturing spirituality.

The most eloquent example of this transforming aspect of grief is contained within this poem written by Joseph Digman to his sister-in-law after her loss.

The Sitting Time

Don't listen to the foolish unbelievers
who say forget.
Take up your armful of roses and
remember them
the flowers and the fragrances.
When you go home to do your sitting
in the corner by the clock
and sip your rosethorn tea.
It will warm your face and fingers
and burn the bottom of your belly.
But as her gone-ness piles in white,
crystal drifts,
it will be the blossom of her moment
the warmth on your belly,
the tiny fingers unfolding,
the new face you've always known,
That has changed you.
Take her moment and hold it
As every mother does.
She will always be your daughter
And when the sitting is done you'll find
bitter grief could never poison
the sweetness of her time.

> (As quoted in Panuthos and
> Romeo 1984, 196)

The same transformation of feeling is worshipfully sung in the Buddhist Psalms of 500 Bereaved Mothers:

Lo! from my heart the hidden shaft is gone,
The shaft that nestled there she hath removed,
And the consuming grief for my dead child
Which poisoned all the life of me is dead.

Now all my sorrows are hewn down, cast out,
Uprooted, brought to utter end,
In that I can now grasp and understand
The base on which my miseries were built.

Change of Values and Greater Tolerance

Knapp's next two typical responses of bereaved parents include a change of values and more tolerance. These two responses, combined with a deepened spirituality, shaped the subsequent character of the individual and family life. Life itself was now viewed as more fragile and thus the family valued activities that nurtured emotional closeness. Jobs, social standing, and monetary gain held less attraction. More aware of the vicissitudes and depth of human sorrow, they reported an increased tolerance for the suffering of others. Knapp acknowledged that he could not assert that this tolerance actually extended to a reduction in "prejudicial" feelings toward other ethnic, racial, or religious groups, but it might be enhanced "if the others were perceived as suffering from hardships over which they have no control." As reflected in the common sentiment, "There but for the grace of God go I," these families had encountered an experience which ultimately enhanced their generosity toward others. Their self-identities now included an understanding of the intensity and depth of human emotion and its ability to disrupt the organization of their daily lives.

Shadow Grief

Knapp's last finding is the frequent presence of "shadow grief." The concept of shadow grief, first developed by Peppers and Knapp in their book *Motherhood and Mourning* (1980), described the lingering effects of grief as suffered by mothers with perinatal losses. As Knapp clarifies it, "Shadow grief is a form of 'chronic' grief that sometimes must be borne for most of their lives. It does not manifest itself overtly, it does not debilitate, no effort is required to cope with it" (Knapp 1986, 40). He adds that it may be characterized as an emotional dullness, a "dull ache in the background of one's feelings." Where shadow grief exists, and it is most prevalent in mothers, individuals can never remember "the events of the loss without feeling some kind of emotion, no matter how mild" (ibid., 41). Although Peppers and Knapp attempt to "normalize" this experience, they nonetheless succumb to a partial pathologizing of it. From my own perspective, their position is logically derived from their ego-dominated approach to the resolution of mourning. By their inference, a full recovery would entail the complete decathexis of the libido from the lost object, thus making the mourner free from the enduring presence of sadness or pain. Rosenblatt, in his examination of a nineteenth-century diarist concluded, however, that although grief is generally thought to diminish (see Figure 1), it more typically seems "to wane gradually *but* be absent some of the time and present others." As illustrated in Figure 2 (from Rosenblatt 1983, 20–21), the "qualitative aspects of grief probably change over time." The frequency of its intrusion into our life, its duration, and its ability to disrupt our functioning does diminish greatly.

Nonetheless, the "intensity of the peaks of emotional experience, even after many years, may remain the same" (ibid., 19–20). Simply put, when we allow ourselves to remember, we may care as much as

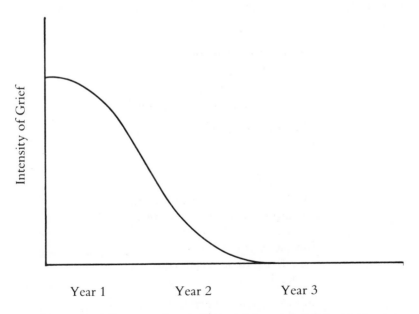

Figure 1. Misconceptions of Diminishment of Grieving in the Process of Grief

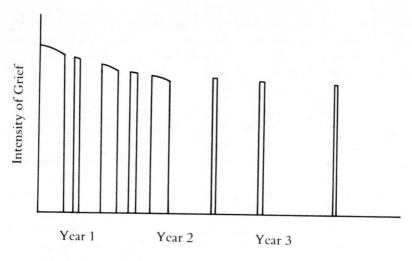

Figure 2. Actuality of Diminishment of Grieving in the Process of Grief

we did then. The long-term intensity of feeling is described by a mother in her poem submitted to the *Loving Arms Newsletter* (vol. III, no. 3).

Thoughts on a Fifth Anniversary

It's true that she is always in
the back of my mind.
But she's not always *on* my mind.

When I think of her now, I
remember her warmly.
I rarely cry any more out of
hurt or anger.

But there are times when something
can throw me right back to that
very day.
And the depth of my feelings of
loss and pain once again equal
the depth of my love for her.

And I cry. And I hurt.
But it reminds me all the more
that she will always be my child,

part of my life, and that she's
special enough to care about.

Time has healed me.
But time has not made me forget.
—Janis Heil

In my opinion, the prevalence of continued shadow grief illuminates the depth of our human interdependence and our intense attachment to others. I will amplify this point further in a later chapter.

In conclusion, the experience of bereavement as reported by the parents who have lost a child illustrates several limitations in our present understanding of normal grief. First, unlike Freud's assertion, the duration of grief is not exclusively dependent on the extent of the repertoire of memories. Child losses have fewer memories, and as in the case of stillborn or neonatal deaths, perhaps none; but their grief is nonetheless intense. More accurately, the cause of grief's emotional intensity is better understood as derived from the psychological meaning attached to the relationship, which is ultimately directed by the Self.

Numerous thanatological psychologists have partly addressed the issue of "meaning" in their work. Parkes (1971, 1972), for example, discussed the changes within the "assumptive world" of the survivor, which he later linked to "identity" and a "view of oneself." Similarly, Woodfield and Viney (in press) developed a concept of "personal construct," which consisted of an individual's system of "constructed interpretations of himself and the events of the world." Horowitz (1976) discussed "latent self-images" that were activated along with "pre-existing attached to the relationship, which is ultimately directed by the ment as a "distintegration of the structure of meaning *unique to the relationship.*"

As evidenced by these approaches, "meaning" is viewed as being exclusively derived from a personalistic history of experiences and the social roles one occupies within society. When questions of a spiritual, teleological, or archetypal nature are raised, they are only partially acknowledged and then relegated to the domain of theology and religion. Thus, the psychological manifestations of the Self, experienced both through the activation of the transcendent function and through the influence of the constellated archetypal motifs upon the mourning process, is not acknowledged. Further, the shared theoretical assumption of the primacy of the ego within these theories leads to an overemphasis on external adaptation which, in some ways, is psychologically tantamount to a regressive restoration of the persona. By "restoration of the persona" I mean a psychological position that denies the loss and the trauma, asserting instead that nothing has changed. The collective emphasis on returning to adequate social functioning, by its own limiting nature, omits a conscious awareness of the restorative capacity of the Self.

In addition Knapp's findings suggest, in my opinion, an archetypal patterning inherent within the mourning process as a whole. As an archetypal motif grief contains dual or opposing aspects which, if they remain unconscious, may threaten the ego through an overidentification with either aspect of its polarity. Such a condition results in the inevitability of an enantiodromia, a psychological condition in which eventually everything turns into its opposite. As Samuels (1986) describes it, "If an extreme, one-sided tendency dominates conscious life, in time an equally powerful counter-position is built up in the psyche" (53). Under the condition of a one-sided ego identification with either pole of the archetypal paradigm (i.e., Good Mother–Bad Mother), an inflation naturally results. Persons experience themselves as having greater power, authority, and responsibility than they realistically possess. Although such identifications and subsequent inflations are generally temporary phases in the mourning process, if they become overly developed a corresponding adjustment of the conscious attitude develops within the unconscious. In this way, the Self, the center of the personality as a whole, seeks to restore balance within the psychic economy. Inherent in grief is the possibility of a restitution within the ego-Self axis. If this restorative aspect is realized, it leads naturally toward a humanizing transformation and expansion within the personality, which Jung called individuation.

Finally, in my opinion, grief is in part enduring. Its resolution need not preclude the continued depth of feeling toward the deceased. It does, however, require an authentic love, achieved through the inner work of psychological differentiation from Self and other and a re-integration of these projections.

From the perspective of a Self psychology, such as Jung's, there exists an inherent tension between the pursuit of individuation and the aims of collectivity. Nonetheless, if the experience of life is approached as potentially revealing the individual's unique nature and the relationship between the conscious and unconscious realms is expanded, the religious or spiritual attitude can be consciously realized.

Chapter 2

The Annunciation:
The Meaning of Progeny

God gave the first man and woman a choice between two kinds of death. They could die like the moon, being reborn over and over again. Or, they could die like the tree, which puts forth new seeds, and, although dying, it lives on through its progeny. It was a difficult decision, but the first man and woman chose to have children even at the cost of their own deaths. And, which of us, asks the storyteller, would not make the same choice?

—Bara Legend, Malayo-Polynesian Culture

The Heart of Mary

Dear sister, I was human not divine,
The angel left me woman as before,
And when, like flame beneath my heart, I bore
The Son, I was the vestal and the shrine.

My arms held Heaven at my breast—not wine
But milk made blood, in which no mothering doubt
Prefigured patterns of the pouring out,
O Lamb! to stain the world incarnadine.

The Magi saw a crown that lay ahead,
But not the bitter glory of the reign;
They called him King and knelt among the kine.
I pondered in my heart what they had said,
Yet could not see the bloody cup of pain.
I was but woman—though my God was mine.

Oxford Sonnets

The Bara folk legend and the preceding poem consolidate the essential mystery inherent in parenthood: Birth and death are inextricably linked. As Jung explained, deep within the psychoid realm of the unconscious where body and psyche unite, death and life converge. As is so poetically described above in "The Heart of Mary," most modern women giving birth cannot see the "cup of pain" poised on the edge of their experience. Mary, the mother of God, has come to symbolize this convergence of Thanatos and Eros in the many representations of herself as mother of the child destined to die. A close scrutiny of the numerous blissful paintings of the Madonna and baby Jesus reveals the fateful outcome presaged either by the small thorn bird poised on Jesus' hand or by the cross, standing silent in the distant background. The famous and dramatic triptych of Colmar, for example, depicts the infant Christ, wrapped in the swaddling clothes of his future tattered shroud, being lovingly gazed upon by his mother. Behind the mother and child stands his future deathbed, draped with the same torn and ancient cloth. However, even for a modern woman the act of childbirth is as close to dying as any human experience approaches.

"To be pregnant and allow the pregnancy to come to term is to permit a process that is alien to oneself to be engaged inside one's body" (Kolbenschlag 1979, 156). Pregnancy has its own rhythm and structure and its own end, which is essentially impersonal. The impersonal aspect of pregnancy is experienced within the instinctual stratum, beyond the awareness of the individual ego, and is shared by the human community of womanhood. Through pregnancy a woman can experience herself as complete in herself and independent of man. The product of her labor, the actual child, according to Harding, "is another Self, a non-personal 'object' Self." Similarly, "the spiritual child, born of the experience of her maternity, is, in the same way, a non-personal, new center of the psyche which Jung calls the Self" (1970, 170).

The elemental nature of the Great Mother archetype constellated with the awareness of pregnancy contains both positive and negative attributes. As positive mother, she is the "vessel" which contains, protects, nourishes, and gives birth; as the negative mother, she is the one who separates, rejects, and brings death. In this capacity, the Great Mother is later associated with the very trauma of birth for the child and with the subsequent existential experiences of rejection which furthered the natural development of the child. As Neumann explains, "This constellation is the foundation of what has been personalistically designated as the 'birth trauma' and interpreted as the cause of all evil" (1963, 66–67). Hillman expresses a similar idea when he states, "The mother archetype itself is responsible for loading the burdens of the archetypal upon personal figures" (1975, 37). To enter the condition of motherhood, a woman's experience extends into this archetypal realm. As Jung observes, we tend to "load the enormous burden of meaning, responsibility, duty, heaven and hell, on the shoulders of one frail and fallible human being . . . who was our mother" (1969b, par. 172).

The Father archetype similarly has dual aspects. As lawgiver, the father is associated with the collective authority and logos. He defends the status quo, embodies activity, penetration, differentiation, judgment, fecundity, and protection. Negatively, he exercises power, destruction, competitiveness, and ruthless aggression (Stevens 1983, 104–108). Unlike the mother archetype, the father constellation is generally activated later in the life of the child when the father enacts his instrumental role of directing the child toward society. In the early stages, however, his fecundity and protection are the more salient features.

Childbearing preserves, biologically, the continuation of the species. Psychologically, the child is also, in part, a completion of the parents, offering them a type of immortality. Children represent futurity, are products of our creativity, symbolize growth and independence (Hillman 1975) and the possibility to live out through them our own unfulfilled potential. Under fortunate circumstances, a child can deepen a marriage, enlarge the scope of the personalities, and enhance the sense of identity. As Harding observes, "many women sense dimly that in the experience of childbirth more happens than they are conscious of" (1970, 170).

According to Lifton, Laski described childbirth as one of several basic human experiences of ecstasy, characterized by a "compelling sense of psychic unity, perceptual intensity, illumination and insight" (Lifton 1983, 25). In a wanted pregnancy, a woman can feel fulfilled as she enacts the creation and bearing of a new life. In Cambodia, a woman who dies with her child in childbirth is said to have died *than klom*, meaning to die completely. She had fulfilled her destiny as a woman and united with her child in death; her spirit remains content. If, however, she dies after a successful delivery, she is said to die *phraaj*, the same name given to the fierce spirits who haunt and harm pregnant women out of envy and disappointment (Rajadhon n.d., 111).

The physical dangers of childbirth are greatly removed from the experience of most modern women. In the process of giving birth, a woman enters a liminal phase, an in-betweenness, balancing between physical life and death and the social shifting of roles and identities. In childbirth the mother moves from girl to the status of motherhood, and the newborn proceeds to the status of a human embodied with a soul (von Gennep 1909). Thus, the primitive concerns regarding death are based not only on the physical dangers but also on an awareness of the "death" of former aspects of one's role within the group. Even in modern woman, it is not uncommon to undergo a phase of mental preoccupation with death imagery, which occurs typically in the last trimester.

At the moment of birth, death and life converge and its participants attentively await the outcome of the instinctual unfolding of the event. In many primitive cultures, death spirits lurk at the door of the labor hut ready to claim the vulnerable spirit of mother and child. Similarly, pregnant tribal women are restricted from certain tribal functions, covered with protective amulets, and housed in special quarters. Birth rituals demand a close adherence to pattern in order to accomplish the successful transition of birth. Following childbirth, many cultures impose a period of seclusion. This seclusion both enhances the bonding between the mother and child and establishes a period of time before the as-yet-vulnerable child is assumed into the community. The length of this period varies within cultures. However, as van Gennep states:

> It logically follows that the children who have not yet been incorporated into the society of the living cannot be classified in that of the dead. . . . The corpse of the semicivilized infant not yet named, circumcised, baptized, or otherwise ritually acknowledged, is buried without usual ceremonies, thrown away or burned—especially if the people in question think that it did not yet possess a soul. (1909, 152–53)

This does not mean, however, that its parents did not grieve. Following the death, the mother would typically undergo a cleansing or purification ritual in order to sever any remaining links with the deceased child and to symbolically reinstate her fertility.

Despite the arrogance of civilized cultures, the primitive practice of disposing of "soul-less" infants without ceremony is not unlike the policies of modern hospitals. Hospitals have only recently, after the protests of parents who had suffered an infant loss, altered their practice of too quickly disposing of the remains, for before that dead infants were rarely named, seen, or even referred to by the staff. Such a practice only compounded the difficulties the mourners had in resolving their grief.

Recently in my community a pro-life group publicly displayed the remains of aborted fetuses, some in the second trimester, which they had allegedly retrieved from a clinic's outdoor trashbin. As Hillman states, "abortion echoes the older practice of child exposure, abandoning the unwanted child to its death" (1975, 38–39). Regardless of our political beliefs on the availability of abortion, our cultural attitude toward the disposal of aborted remains reveals the nature of our collective relationship to the shadow aspects of the child archetype. Although western society has long been fascinated by the archetypal child motif, our attraction is fixated upon its positive aspects of youthfulness, vitality, innocence, growth, potential, and openness (Hillman 1975). Conversely, negative images related to the child motif, such as regression, stasis, madness, and primitivity, are ignored (ibid.). Together they compose the collective shadow of this archetypal motif. The cavalier disposal of remains and the blatant refusal to ackncowledge the loss reveal our collective anger and disappointment, which is then projected onto the "defective" child. It is not uncommon for doctors or nursing staff to regard an infant death as revealing their personal limitations and weaknesses. As Kennell, Slyter, and Klaus explain:

> The insensitive struggle for life now practiced in most neonatal units has some of the spirit of a sports arena, where a loss is almost unacceptable. When death occurs, not only the physician, but every member of the obstetrical team is touched by a sense of defeat and the urgent desire to pin the blame elsewhere. (1970)

This same denial of the loss is also a common response of relatives and friends. Oriana Fallaci writes in her novel *Letters to a Child Never Born*:

> They greeted me with great enthusiasm, as though I'd been sick with a foot or ear ailment and was now beginning to convalesce. They congratulated me for carrying my work through to the end despite-the-difficulties. They took me out to eat. And never a word about you. When I tried to say something, they assumed an expression between evasiveness and embarrassment: almost as though I were bringing up a disagreeable subject and they wanted to say let's-not-think-about-it-any-more-what-has-been-has-been. (1975, 108)

The body of the dead infant symbolizes the "miscarriage of archetypal hopes for a future, the sense of conquest, the new start, and the fulfilled end" from which we wish to turn away (Hillman 1975, 39). The acts of holding, gazing, naming, and ceremoniously burying are themselves archetypal expressions of parental attachment and bonding. The enactment of these acts attributes to the child a soul, an identity, and, as such, aids in the survivor's comprehension of the loss and facilitates mourning. Contrary to the common expectation, embracing the dead infant is not too emotionally painful to bear. Rather, the observed pattern was for parents to examine the baby closely and in detail, noting family resemblances. Lewis described how a mother of a premature baby who died after ten days in an incubator responded when told she could now hold the dead child. "With great excitement she stripped off his clothes, kissed him all over, and then walked him on the floor. Soon afterward, she calmed down and handed the dead baby back to the nurse" (Lewis 1976, 619–20). This process enabled the parents to incorporate the baby as a tangible love object and then separate from it. Without such an enactment, the dead child exerted a ghostly pull on the survivors. Parents, particularly mothers, search desperately for images of what the baby would have looked like. Other infants of approximately the same age would often be compared for possible similarities. Denying this psychological need to incarnate the child in image only brings these mothers further into the nonadaptive realms of fantasy and wish fulfillment. Overall, the natural process of mourning is complicated if such attachments are not allowed expression (Peppers and Knapp 1980).

Parents I have spoken with have frequently discussed the importance of such remembrances as photos of the deceased child, birth certificates complete with the imprints of tiny feet, naming the child, or holding a funeral or memorial service for him or her. In correspondence or discussion, almost all parents felt that being allowed to hold the child or in other ways give psychological reality to its life was helpful to them. The following poem, presented as part of the annual memorial service conducted by the local Pregnancy and Infant Loss Center, addresses this very real need.

Farewell Song to Baby

Pretty baby, so small, so sweet,
You've made your parents' love complete.

A lock of hair I clipped away
And the bracelet of life though in death you lay.

No baby steps will run to meet—
The only prints of your tiny feet
Are on this card that shows your name,
Souvenirs, all, that show you came.

A sorrowed vigil with tears we keep
Your parents and I together weep.

Cuddled close are you, while they
Kiss you goodbye on your birthing day.
—Pat Thorlson

Similarly, in primitive cultures, the lack of attributing soul or of performing the customary funeral rituals condemned the deceased to a pitiful fate. As van Gennep explains,

> *Like children who have not been baptized, named or initiated, persons for whom funeral rites are not performed are condemend to a pitiful existence, since they are never able to enter the world of the death or become incorporated within the society established there. These (entities) are the most dangerous of the dead. They would like to be reincorporated into the world of the living, and since they cannot be, they behaved like hostile strangers toward it.* (1909, 160)

The concern of bereaved parents for the well-being of the child's soul or spirit is a common occurrence. Fearing that they had abandoned or neglected the child because they were not given the opportunity to ritually acknowledge its birth and death, their bereavement is complicated. Although Western culture no longer believes in ghosts or spirits, the so-called primitive belief in them is a powerful metaphor for the continuing effect of the child's loss upon the parent. As the van Gennep quotation illustrates, the spirit of the child needs acknowledgment or it continues to exert a powerful influence from the world of the dead.

One of the unique features of infant bereavement is that the loss occurs at the height of psychological bonding. The bonding behavior of parents toward a child begins sooner than is commonly acknowledged. It usually occurs int he mother somewhere in the second trimester when the quickening of the fetus is first experienced. With this occurrence, the fetus begins to emerge as a separate identity from the mother. In contrast, as the father's awareness of his wife's pregnanat condition increases, his identification with the paternal roles as provider and protector also increases.

With the awareness of the "otherness" of the new life within her, conflicts begin to surface in the mother between the wished-for child and the enemy within. This phase is described by Erickson as an inner space that is at once "fulfillment and despair." As Kolbenschlag explains, "Children, even wanted ones, represent the most serious threat to personal autonomy and, at the same time, the most significant bridge to theonomous selfhood" (1979, 155). Such natural doubts have a heightened importance in childbearing losses. It is common for

parents to fear that any ambivalence regarding the pregnancy contributed to its failure. The focus of the mother's concern at this early stage
is captivated by the physical changes occurring within her. She may
experience a slight estrangement from herself, a feeling of loneliness
and distance from others. She is struck by the idea of a chain of generations and of herself as a link between the past and future (Harding 1970;
Hall 1980).

The bonding behavior now activated within the parents, particularly
within the mother, is best understood as a type of *participation mystique*.
Adult bonding, although less instinctually rigid than the infant's corresponding attachment behavior, is nonetheless a compelling, a priori,
dynamic "at work in the (mother's) phylogenetic psyche" (Stevens
1983, 89).

Mothers, and fathers too, begin with the knowledge of pregnancy,
the process of attachment to the child by the means of projection.
Images of the child's appearance begin to form in the minds of its
parents, with parental genetic attributes being imagined as belonging to
the child. The infant may be thought to possess the father's color of
hair, or the mother's eyes. For the most part, these images are idealized, representing healthy and happy infants. They can, however, represent a fearful attitude toward the child, as illustrated by the pictures
below. The psychic reality of these images is clear in the illustrations
provided by Klaus and Kennell (1983, 57). Similarly, parents who gave
birth to deformed or impaired children experienced postpartum depression directly related to the cognitive dissonance created between the
internal images of their child and the actual appearance of their child, as
illustrated in Figure 3.

To understand the quality of the human bond between parent and
child, we must also consider the influence of the spontaneous constellation of archetypal imagery inherent in the collective unconscious of the
human psyche. Ideas similar to the concept of archetype are also
described by Lifton and include his own concept of inchoate images
(1983), Langer (1942) (symbologist school of philosophy), Portman
(1964) ("inner world" or "realm of images" within lower forms of life),
Cameron (1963) (active central nervous system representation), and
Boulding (1956) (pattern structures), to name a few. The inner images
or motifs of child, mother, father, and family, are shaped not only by
personalistic factors, but also, most certainly, by the character of archetypal imagos related to them. As Jung and later Hillman stress, these
imagos are "composed of dual aspects, or tandems, and thus can only
be accurately comprehended by a grasping of the dynamic interaction

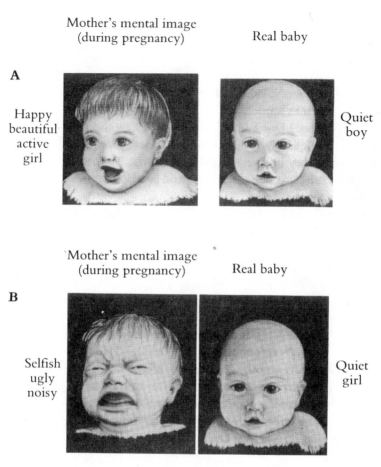

Figure 3. A. The mental image of the baby this mother planned to have is completely different from the baby she has. **B**. The mental image for some women with mothering disorders and the real infant.

between the opposites as well as the autonomy of each aspect of these opposing poles." Thus, Hillman explains, for example, that "we assume that there is an inner child, an archetypal child imago, affecting each of us and so affecting every mother and mothering act" (Hillman 1983, 166).

Regarding the concept of archetype, Jung, according to Samuels, originally "connected the archetype and its functions to the instincts," first seeing it as a "psychological analogue to the instinct" or "the instinct's perception of itself" (1985, 27). Later, according to Samuels, Jung revised his proposition that archetypes were "instinctual correlates" and distinguished them as fundamental and equal to the instincts themselves. The archetype is equivalent to a "structured predisposition" that then seeks its correspondence within the external environment. Without such external correspondence, archetypes, or rather their images, would not be realized within consciousness. Through the concept of the autonomous nature of the archetype, as manifested by the constellation of the complex, Jung linked the "collective and the personal realms" (*ibid.*, 47). Lastly, archetypes themselves are distinguished from their images or motifs. Archetypal images are observed in myth, literature, fairy tale, folklore, religion, and other forms of human expression. However, the archetype as such, according to Jung, "never was conscious and never will be . . . and it was, and still is, only interpreted" (1969*b*, par. 266). Archetypal images manifest themselves throughout the mechanism of projection.

Jung, in writing on alchemy, stated:

> *Strictly speaking, projection is never made; it happens, it is simply there. In the darkness of anything external to me I find, without recognizing it as such, an interior or psychic life which is my own.* (1968b, par. 346)

This quotation describes the natural process of the projection of the archetypal image within the human psyche and the subsequent need to become conscious of these projections, thus reintegrating them as aspects of one's own psyche. This psychological process and its relationship to mourning will be addressed in more detail in a later section of this work.

The images of the parents' fantasy of themselves in the role of parent and the internal image of their unborn child are a complex amalgam of personal experiences of childhood and the quality of the past relationship with the original parents. These images are further shaped by the collective values assigned to the role of parenthood. As has already been discussed, although many modern psychologists acknowledge the natural construction of image within the psyche, their analysis is typically confined to the personal and collective contributions to image formation. Thus, as Hillman describes, our connection to the history of mankind is ignored, which results in an egocentric interpretation of the psyche. Referring to Corbin, Hillman adds that archetypal psychology "returns to the higher principle in order to find place for and understand the lesser" (1983). The conscious desire to become a family, combined with the onset of pregnancy, activates the psychobiologic, archetypal realm of the collective unconscious, thereby producing its corresponding imagery. For most families seeking a wanted child, their conscious attention is captivated by the positive aspects of the archetypal motifs as related to the mother, father, child, and family.

In pregnancy, a woman begins to imagine herself as a nurturing, loving mother to her future newborn child. Her experience of pregnancy can often bring her closer to her own mother, toward whom she may now be more tolerant and with whom she might now gain the emotional connection with the generations of mothers before her. She readies the nursery and takes pleasure in collecting tiny pink or blue clothing. And at a baby shower she, along with all kinds of women—feminist and nonfeminists alike—cannot help but succumb to the spontaneous oohs and aahs as they giggle unrestrainedly at the cuteness of the tiny things—testimony to the power of the captivating divine-child motif.

However, not only the positive aspects of the mother imago are felt. Many women experience the somatic, psychoid level of the physicality of pregnancy. Thus, body and self-concept issues can interrupt the peaceful maternity with fears of "growing fat" or "unattractive," or fear over the blood and the pain of childbirth. As I have already stated, by the last trimester many women become aware of an increasingly morbid preoccupation. However, for most women, this morbidity is pushed away or dismissed since it understandably disrupts the otherwise positive quality of the maternal experience.

The father's relation to the positive aspect of the father constellation is manifested as a proud, potent fecundity. Later, as the wife becomes more visibly pregnant, he may identify with his role as protector, ever solicitous of his wife's condition and concerned with his responsibilities as breadwinner. On the negative side, he can, however, become like Kronos, jealous and competitive for his wife's attentions, and his moody demandingness for sexual or emotional attention may threaten to almost devour the mother and child (Harding 1970).

As for the child, the parents evolve an inner image most often typified by the archetypal motif of the Divine Child. Rarely can one find a new parent who does not assert, "Isn't he/she the cutest baby you ever saw?" Nonetheless, the tranquility of the parental joy is occasionally disturbed by images of demanding, crying, colicky babies, or, more dramatically, by ideas of injury, handicap, deformity, or death.

Lastly, given that the child is genuinely desired, even if for narcissistic reasons, parents find themselves musing on the thoughts of fulfillment, completion, expansion, growth, multiplicity, generativity, and other positive aspects inherent within the archetypal motif of the family. The spiritual association with the family archetype is envisioned, most notably, in the Christian imagery of the Holy Family. Nestled within the sanctity of the moment, the holy parents focus their loving attention on the tiny babe lying in the manger. The Star of Bethlehem illuminates the scene with a divine radiance, and wise men have traveled far to witness the birth of Jesus. It is within this heightened moment of ecstasy and fulfillment that the shocking and unnatural death of the infant occurs. Even with the loss of older children, the immediacy and intensity of this familial Holy Family constellation is still operative. Death robs the parents of their opportunity to live it to completion. For parents who have suffered a child loss, a dark and tragic journey of mourning begins.

Chapter 3

Ethnological and Archetypal Motifs Governing the Structure of Mourning

Archetypal images need to be divested of their power and autonomy by a "changing of names"; they must be rendered intelligible
on the personal level and a polarization between "numinous" and
awe-inspiring and commonplace be avoided. If this happens, if
the ego can manage such integration, then the personality is enriched.

— Andrew Samuels, *Jung and the Post-Jungians*

Ethnological Data Relevant to the
Collective Patterning of Mourning

According to Gorer: "There are very few universal traits or practices
found in all human society. . . . Among them are rules and rituals
concerning the disposal of the dead and the appropriate behavior of the
mourners" (1973, 423–24). Bowlby adds that "in some societies, the
funeral is the most important of all social ceremonies in terms of the
numbers present and its duration" (1980, 126). Summarizing the work
of R. Firth, Bowlby states that the funeral serves three distinct ends: (1)
helping the bereaved, (2) taking note of the loss, (3) providing an
occasion for the complex interchange of goods and services. Bowlby
adds to these observations two other collective objectives: to provide an
opportunity for the living to express gratitude to the deceased and to

provide the opportunity to take some further action felt to be of benefit to the deceased (*ibid.*, 127).

Death ceremonies further serve as rites of passage (van Gennep 1909). Thus, the death is followed by a passage ceremony and the deceased is "removed from the world of the living to the symbolic world of the dead" (Rosenblatt et al. 1976). For the mourner, "such ceremonies facilitate the transition from one's previous roles and statuses, no longer appropriate in light of the death, toward new statuses and roles" (*ibid.*, 128).

Other functional attributes of such ceremonies include structures that define a permissible period of mourning. These would include any form of anniversary celebration or a burial subsequently followed by a later and final ceremony. Such ceremonies may coincide with annual feasts; others with a final disposition of the remains and the termination of acceptable expressions of grief.

According to Bowlby, almost all societies believe "that despite a bodily death, the person not only lives on but continues his relationship with the living at least for a time" (1980, 128). Similarly, Rosenblatt, Walsh, and Jackson concluded in their cross-cultural study that it is "fundamentally human to have ghost cognitions and to respond to familiar stimuli in ways that would only be appropriate if the deceased were still alive" (1976, 49). As Bowlby clarifies it, "Failure to recognize that a continuing sense of the dead person's presence is a common feature of healthy mourning has led to much confused theorizing" (1980, 100). This confusion has caused a blurring in the understanding of healthy and pathological mourning, most often attributing ghost cognitions to a pathological condition. Such ghost cognitions are also common in infant loss. Many parents reported later responding to the cries of infants other than their own, even though they may never have actually heard their own child cry. Another frequent occurrence is the lingering post-natal sensation of fetal movement. Sherokee Ilse, author of *Empty Arms*, writes,

> *Often I feel what I believe is my baby kicking. At first I thought that was very strange and I worried about my sanity. After talking with other mothers, I found that this was very common, and I was relieved. I am not so afraid of these sensations now, and in fact, I try to remember the joyful times associated with those kicks.* (1982, 26)

Regarding the collective ritual, Neumann states that it is essential for the life of the community. Ritual is the product of the "group self, . . . a self which is also operative in the single individual but which exceeds its limited world-time-space" (1976, 6). Such rituals, according to him, evolve through a fundamental archetypal patterning having its origin in the *archetype of the way*. This archetypal patterning is made manifest through the group's compulsion to follow the ritualistic observances even though the rituals may pose potential risk or danger to the individual (e.g., circumcision). Secondly the ritual reflects the tendency toward consciousness that is present in all of us. The superior wisdom "toward which all ritual is directed is, by itself, sufficiently powerful to overcome anxiety and fear and compels the members of the group to penetrate even the most fearsome of spaces or events" (*ibid.*, 9). The intended culmination of all ritual is a transformation.

As previously stated, it is common to experience, at least for a time, the ongoing presence of the deceased. Thus, depending on the cultural attitude toward such an experience, that is, whether the presence of such spirits is collectively regarded as beneficial or detrimental, most cultures provide for a social sanction of these phenomena, and appropriate behavior in relation to them is prescribed (Rosenblatt, Walsh, and Jackson 1976). On the more contemporary end of phenomenological research, the observation of the normal experience of a continuing felt presence of the deceased also holds. As already discussed, Parkes's study of London widows found the last two of four basic mourning processes to include

> *. . . processes that maintain a belief that loss is not permanent and that reunion is still possible; and secondly, processes that result in recognition that loss has in fact occurred* combined *with a feeling that the links with the dead manifested often in a comforting sense of the continuing presence of the lost person.* (As quoted in Bowlby, 1980, 140)

Bowlby agrees that the discriminating factor in the judgment of these experiences as pathological rests exclusively with two factors: the length of time they persist and the extent to which they dominate other aspects of mental functioning. Otherwise, they must be wholly regarded as a part of healthy mourning.

According to von Franz, Jung originally regarded the spirits of the dead as projected inner images. He later revised his position and "was no longer quite sure that spirits are only such personal images, possessing no reality of their own" (1980, 104–5). This, according to Jung, "opens up the whole question of the transpsychic reality immediately underlying the unconscious" (Jung 1969a, par. 600). Von Franz elaborates that psychologically this means "simply that the images of the spirits of the dead are gradually assimilated into collective archetypal images. The psychic energy that clings to the memory image of the deceased charges an image in the collective unconscious which is thereby activated" (1980, 105). However, the question raised here with its far-reaching implications of the reality of reincarnation or immortality is beyond the scope of this work.

As with all collective, ritualistic productions, individuals express more conformity than not in their expressions of bereavement. Thus, it is with relative assurance that each of us can assume a general understanding and expectation of what bereavement would behaviorally include. In a previous chapter I discussed several typical responses to grieving as experienced by the parents in Knapp's study. Now I wish to return again to the phenomenology of mourning so that I may examine more closely the archetypal motifs observable within these human behaviors. I do not intend to entirely exhaust the vast range and vicissitudes of mourning behavior, but I do intend to amplify those characteristics that are both clearly archetypal in kind and relevant to the topic at hand: childbearing losses.

The basis of my examination of the patterning of grief rests primarily on one rather uncomplicated idea: That the mourning process in its entirety, including the period of time extending beyond the behaviors of overt mourning, is a cryptic analogue for the process of individuation—a process that otherwise unfolds throughout a lifetime. Machtiger expressed the same idea when she stated, "The bereavement process can be seen as synonymous with ego development and the differentiation of the psyche. The symbolic attitudes emerge only after this psychic differentiation has occurred" (1985, 106).

As Mario Jacoby eloquently describes it, the individuation process "is the individual experience of 'death and rebirth' through struggle and suffering, through a conscious, lifelong, unremitting endeavor to broaden the scope of one's consciousness and so attain a greater inner freedom" (1965, 62).

Individuation is, however, not equivalent to the better known concept of individuality and as such does not refer only to the process of establishing an ego–identity. Rather, its essence culminates in "the achievement of a personal blend between the collective and universal, on the one hand, and on the other, the unique and individual" (Samuels 1985, 101). Ultimately, it is a movement toward wholeness which is directed by the central and organizing archetype of the psyche—the Self.

Neumann's Archetype of the Way as a Paradigm for Mourning

The theoretical, or more accurately, the metaphorical structure of my analysis is derived from Neumann. First, it is predicated upon what Neumann describes as the *archetype of the way*. The choice of this archetypal configuration is appropriate on several counts. As a central archetypal image of the structure and intent of ritual, "it contains a number of essential analogies to the instincts but is also rooted" (Neumann 1976, 8) in the phenomenon of human ritual. Animals, as well as man, perform rituals. Neumann describes these "quasi-rituals" as "the instinctual direction of drives toward the maintenance of and life defense of the individual creature." He adds, however, that even within this substratum, "something else is at work which directs the transformation or metamorphosis of the animal" (*ibid.*, 1), such as from a chrysalis to butterfly. Secondly, the archetype of the way evokes a similar transformation in human ritual. As Neumann states, "Ritual, we may note, was first conceived of as a *way*, and even today one 'walks' or celebrates a ritual" (*ibid.*, 8). Thus, the compelling prospect of transformation, as offered through the enactment of ritual, outweighs, for example, the dangers of initiation rites among primitive man. Guided by its transformative intent, ritual requires of the participants a religious attitude. As Hillman describes it, "Because the religious moment requires a passive mood to God's intention, a receptive state to Divine Will, a wounding experience which opens us, it is feminine in nature" (1967, 108).

As a central metaphor for mourning, the archetype of the way evokes the dangerous darkness inherent in enactment of many primitive rituals and is thus affectually analogous to the grievous and frightening experience of mourning (e.g., dark depressions, suicide, self-recrimination, or mutilation). Secondly, despite a conscious wish to not enter the awesome psychic territory of mourning, man is driven there nonetheless. Like ancient man's initiation mysteries, grief also seeks to understand and experience the healing, transformative nature of the numinous. As Neumann explains, "Fascination with the archetype which contains as much attraction as repulsion, and as much anxiety and horror, leads man—and this is the essential point—not to flight but to penetration" (1976, 9).

My second metaphorical analogy to the process of mourning is the archetypal paradigm of mourning as enacted by the Goddess. As Neumann describes it, this process proceeds from *birth* to *death*, and is followed by *search, recovery* and *rebirth* (1970). This paradigm is enacted in the myths of such goddesses and their lost son/lovers or daughters as Innana and Dumuzi, Demeter and Persephone, Isis and Osiris, and, more recently, Mary and Christ. In the following material I will attempt to amplify this archetypal paradigm with the human experience of mourning to add to my already existing discussion of the constellation of archetypal identifications within the psyche of the bereaved parent. Lastly, as is tragically the case with the families of this study, the first two phases of this process have already transpired. There was a birth and, too shortly thereafter, death.

Thus the archetypal configuration of the *search* begins.

Chapter 4

Archetypal Patterns of Mourning:
The Search

Once, ritual lament would have been chanted; women would have been paid to beat their breasts and howl for you all night, when all is silent. Where can we find such customs now? So many have long since disappeared or been disowned. That's what you have come for: to retrieve the lament that we omitted. Can you hear me? I would like to fling my voice out like a cloth over the fragments of your death, and keep pulling at it until it is torn to pieces, and all my words would have to walk around shivering, in the tatters of that voice; if lament were enough.

  Rainer Maria Rilke, "Requiem," *Duino Elegies*, 1923

Although most research and the experience of mourning describe an undeniable period of shock, denial, disbelief, or numbing, these periods are, overall, relatively transient. However, because of their intensity, this initial period understandably receives much attention. At this stage, the mourner is generally comforted by the ready emotional support of friends and family, who try to direct the mourner's attention toward funeral and other arrangements. The mourner's open expression of sadness is collectively tolerated. Lasting a few days or weeks, the denial mechanisms eventually loosen and the mourner begins to accept the reality of the loss. Together, these varied and intense early emotional reactions to the loss combine to create, as in the first phase of any initiation ritual, a period of disorganization or disorientation within the conscious personality. The following stage, that of Searching, also known as Yearning or Longing, is more enduring and is particularly distressful to parents, especially mothers, who have lost children. Phe-nomenologically, this period is experienced as an unyielding ache in the mother's empty arms, or an intense heartache as symbolized by the Seven Swords presaged by Simeon that would pierce the heart of Mary, the Mother of Jesus, following his crucifixion. The behaviors of mourning that are constellated by the archetype of the Search include wandering, cutting of hair, dressing in black, being "unkempt," and relentlessly weeping. Its affects include depression, crying, anger, confusion, and pain.

Wandering, Searching, Hair Cutting, Unkempt Appearance

Isis

In the Isis-Osiris myth (as related by Plutarch), Nut, the Mother of the Gods, is secretly united with Seb (Time). When Ra, her spouse, and the Sun discover this, he curses that she cannot "bring forth" within any given day or month. Nut seeks the help of Thoth (order) who creates five extra days. On the first day Osiris was born, on the second, the Elder Horus, the third, Set, the fourth, Isis, and on the fifth, her sister Nephthys. Isis and Osiris have intercourse in their mother's womb, which, it is related, produced the Elder Horus. Osiris is killed by Set and later his death is avenged by his son, the Elder Horus. Set tricks Osiris to fall into a custom-made casket, which he then sets adrift in the Nile.

When Isis hears of this, she cuts her hair, puts on a mourning dress, and searches for the casket. In her search she meets the Queen's maidens and then becomes the nurse to the Queen's son, Maneros. She burns the child to give him immortality, but, when stopped by the Queen, demands Osiris' casket. She leaves, taking the child with her, who then "swoons away" when Isis opens the casket and grieves for the dead Osiris. Isis hides the coffin and goes to seek help. Set then finds the coffin and tears the body into 14 pieces and scatters them. Isis returns and searches for the parts, finding all of them except the phallus. She welds the 13 parts together and conse-crates a surrogate phallus with which she conceives the Younger Horus. This Horus, however, is lame. Osiris, then reborn, trains the Elder Horus to seek his revenge. Horus fights Set and is victor. When Horus brings the fallen Set to Isis, she releases him, although she does weaken his strength. Angered by this action, Horus then tears off the head of Isis. Thoth then replaces her head with a cow's head and thus, she becomes the Horned Crescent Hathor.

As the myth states, Isis, in her grieving, laments the death of Osiris. Black-robed, she cuts her hair and wanders, weeping. The cutting of hair is a custom typically related to mourning and sacrifice. The hair, representing energy and fertility, when cut corresponds with the literal lack of fertility. This is observed in Demeter's grief for Persephone, which resulted in her ravaging the Grecian soil with drought (Berry-Hillman 1982). Consequently, the cutting of hair symbolizes an entropaic state, the psychological period prior to a new development in which there exists an inadequate tension between the opposing forces in the energetic psychic field. These opposing forces are most simply understood as the tension between personal ego wants or needs and archetypal Self desires that are aimed at restoration within the ego-Self axis. It is equivalent psychologically to an energetic stagnation. Still clinging to the hopes of being reunited with the lost child, the grieving parents at this stage are yet unable to comprehend the meaning of the loss or to psychologically separate from the child's image. They cannot let go, lest the child be lost forever. This period is reflected in a recurring dream which I received from a mother:

> My older sister, who is an OB nurse at the hospital where I delivered and was present at my son's birth, came to my house one day after work with a Petri dish with the remains of my son. Very matter-of-factly she said, "Well, they're done with the autopsy and this is all that was left. I thought you might want it." With that, her cat jumped on the table, knocked over the dish and started licking the remains of my son. Needless to say, I always woke up screaming.

The dream is made understandable by the horrific nature of this woman's loss. Her son died *in utero* seven weeks before his due date. She carried him for two weeks knowing that he was dead. After inducing labor, she delivered his dead body into the world. In her letter she added, "I never saw him or held him, which to this day I still regret. But, I was too afraid he would be ugly or had started to deteriorate." The dream reveals her struggle in letting go. The sister, a shadow figure, symbolizes the detached, impersonal aspect of the mother archetype, which this dreamer has not yet consciously discovered in herself. Regarding this same theme, Hillman discusses, how the possessive aspect of the mother archetype is compensated by the image of the nurse. Just as with this dreamer's matter-of-fact nurse/sister, the archetype of the nurse "is not personally connected to the child, its life and death is not hers." He adds, "We should not assume the nurse to be a foster mother, a substitute . . . but the nurse is obliged to accept the child as it is . . . and she connects to the plight of abandonment [of the child] in a different way" (1975, 37).

The Isis parallels within this dream are twofold. First, Isis herself embodies some aspects of the nurse archetype. As nurse, she re-members the dismembered body of Osiris. As Hillman explains: "Primarily, the injury, illness, and exposure are met with the nursing instinct, binding up, repairing, protection, as are her acts" (1975, 37). Secondly, the devouring all-motherness of Isis is also represented by the cat who eats the child's remains. It is well known that cats were sacred to Isis and often associated with her. In this aspect of the mother archetype, the dreamer is "mother-cat" which, because of its ego-dystonic character, however, is projected onto the sister shadow. Thus, we can sense dimly this woman's budding awareness that her own grief is devouring, yet, at this juncture, she is unable to free herself from it. Like Osiris, the dismembered remains of the son are displayed (in the Petri dish), and this mother, like Isis, psychologically seeks to bring him back to life again.

Typical to the early phase of grief, as illustrated by the preceding dream and the Isis myth itself, the loss of the child produces a regression into a condition of all-motherness, and, correspondingly, even a man regresses into infancy. This regression is seen in the Isis-Osiris myth:

> She made to rise up the helpless members of him whose heart was at rest. She drew from him his essence and she made therefrom an heir. She suckled the child in solitariness and none knew where his place was.
> (Budge 1973, p. 74)

This "infantalizing" dynamic, and I do not mean this pejoratively, is common to parents who have lost older, even adult, children. They recall with vivid detail their son or daughter as a small child and nurture that image with an inner protective parental solicitousness. So strong is this parental urge that parents of dead adult children cannot help but feel they could have prevented the death through warning, caution, or parental authority. This is clear in the words of these parents: "If only I had insisted on his taking our car that night instead of his, he would not have stopped at that station!" (19-year-old son randomly shot down as an innocent bystander during a holdup); "If only I had cautioned him more diligently about riding with strangers . . ." (16-year-old son brutally beaten and murdered while hitchhiking) (Knapp 1986, 100).

As any parent of adolescent or adult children can attest, parental authority and protectiveness at this stage in life is often overtly disregarded by the child. Too much protectiveness, in fact, runs contrary to the child's evolving sense of independence and adulthood healthy to adolescent development. Regardless of the parents' consciousness of this fact, the child's death remains experienced, on some level, as a failure of their parental protection.

Similar feelings of guilt and failure have been previously mentioned as common to parents who suffered childbearing losses. Mothers such as my analysand Sally scour their memories for forgotten actions that might have caused the child's death. Similarly, another mother with whom I spoke explained, "I had done everything right: quit smoking, exercised, regularly but not too vigorously, ate the right foods, slept the required eight hours a night, and still I'm haunted by the idea I had done something wrong. This idea was so intense, I used to think I saw the accusation in my husband's eyes. But when I'd ask him, he always looked surprised and said he knew it wasn't my fault that the umbilical cord had strangled our baby."

Patty's feelings of guilt and inadequacy after losing both of her twin daughters in the 22nd week of pregnancy were expressed in a recurring dream she had after the birth of another child. Her twins had died because Patty had a rare conditon known as PolyHydramios, a thinning of the umbilical cord, causing one of her children to die at birth and the other 44 hours after delivery. Patty felt responsible for the failed pregnancy. These feelings were compounded by her being asked to make the decision to terminate life supports on the barely surviving daughter. Since the daughter's prognosis was hopeless it was thought that she should not be allowed to suffer. Despite the urgings of the medical staff, the priest, and her husband, Patty could not bring herself to do this. "I just couldn't do it," she explained, "it felt like killing her. It was a critical point in my marriage. I left my husband to do it."

After the birth of another daughter, Patty dreamed:

My husband is holding Kelsey, a seven-pound baby who is happy as a clam and so am I. But I am holding this tiny two-pound baby, and I am trying to get her to the hospital. But the hospital is closed. Nobody helps me. The baby's blanket keeps coming undone, unwrapping, and the baby cries and kicks when I try to wrap it again. The baby is naked.

The dream, which Patty had recurrently, evokes the feeling of helplessness that Patty felt at the death of her twins. Now the mother of a healthy baby, her fears resurfaced. Would she fail this daughter as well?

As suggested by the dream, Patty could not turn her full attention toward her new child until she was freed from the feelings of helplessness and inadequacy constellated by the previous loss. Patty associated her husband, not herself, with having had the courage to make the decision to terminate life support on their twin. She feared she had failed the child and allowed her to suffer. Thus, the dream depicts Patty's husband as the one holding Kelsey, and Patty as the one taken up with the frustrated attempt to get help for the two-pound premature infant. Through the dream Patty is reminded of her helplessness and, by depicting it, puts the dreamer into sympathy with this aspect of herself.

The desire to resurrect the deceased or fragile child is also observed in the following dream provided by Wendy, a woman whose premature infant died *in utero*. The mother reported that "for a long time I had dreams about tiny babies, like ours, that you could fit in your hand." Although the content of the dreams varied some, they typically consisted of the following theme:

> *I dream of small babies, who couldn't possibly live. Somehow, I am always able to feed them with my breast-milk and they grew and grew. Sometimes they were someone else's tiny baby, but the mother was not there. They always were girls. I would initially feel upset and confused, but as the baby began to assume normal size, I would be filled with joy and contentment.*

These dreams clearly serve a compensatory purpose, depicting the mother as having the capacity to nurse her child back to life. The potency of her breast-milk associates the dream ego with the archetypal, regenerative capacity of the Great Mother. The Virgin Mary's milk, for example, represented the gift of life. In her representation as *Maria lactans*, Mary is historically associated with Isis, who suckled Horus. As quoted by Warner, the milk of the Goddess "is truly virginal, the nectar of the spiritual life, through which death meets its defeat" (1976, 199).

The compensatory imagery of this dream serves to disengage the dreamer from her feelings of inadequacy as a mother who had been unable to prevent the death of her child. It is interesting to note how important it was for Wendy to remain true to the spirit of motherhood in spite of the child's death. Although her child's death was discovered after 18 weeks, she refused the general procedure of a D & C. Instead, she elected to have her labor induced so that she could give birth to the child without having its small body dismembered. In this way, Wendy

felt that she and her husband could experience the natural birth together. Because of this decision she later was able to hold their tiny
child, "soft, shiny and brown, but obviously preciously and perfectly
formed in the palm of my hand."

As with Isis, Mary, the Mother of Jesus, also expressed her torment
at Christ's death. Although not typically visually depicted as unkempt
or mad with grief, several poems and verses describe this aspect of the
grieving mother, known as the *Mater Dolorosa* (Mother of Sorrows). In
this representation, she is an emotionally moving force to the believer,
as is attested by the Marian Cults which continue to thrive against the
objection of the traditional church fathers. In a poem in a form called
kontakion, Mary cries out:

> I am overwhelmed, o my son
> I am overwhelmed by love
> And I cannot endure
> That I should be in the chamber
> And you on the wood of the cross
> I in the house
> And you in the tomb.
> (Warner 1976, 209)

This verse parallels the experience of grieving parents who, like
Mary, cannot endure the injustice of the child's death while they themselves survive. As has already been discussed, this feeling often results
in ideas of suicide aimed at making restitution for the unnatural event
of surviving one's progeny. These parents, like Mary in the preceding
kontakion, cannot help but question the meaning of the divine plan.
Sacrifice, an archetypically generated response to death, is present in the
ancient custom of ritually sacrificing either a life or a valued object,
aimed at ameliorating the dissatisfaction of the gods. However, to be
regenerative, such sacrifice must be done consciously, otherwise, as
Jung states, "It is merely an accident, not a moral act" (1939, 129). The
doubt in the benevolence of the deity, activated by the child's death,
then constellates within the parent the urge toward self-sacrifice. In
some cases suicide is considered, in others less dramatic self-sacrifices
may be enacted, as when parents may undervalue the needs of their
bodies and fail to eat or sleep, risking collapse or disease. Sleep does not
come easily. As one parent described it, "I want to sleep. Lord knows I
need sleep. But when I get into bed my mind starts racing. I see her
lifeless body and I think, Why? Why did my body send her out too
soon?" This quotation reveals the psychological reality that the wom-

an's body, itself, is perceived as the cause which results in a variety of later problems in body image and caring for its needs. The heightened kinetic condition of childbirth combined with the powerful associations of corruptibility as experienced in a death have a powerful subjective influence on the survivors. Caring for one's physical needs can also be experienced as a betrayal of the dead child. If the baby was thought to have suffered, then so must the loyal and devout parent. The somatic problems of the survivor will be expanded on in a subsequent part of this chapter.

The cutting of hair, wearing of old or unkempt clothing, wandering unprotected, and the use of the color black to depersonalize the mourner's identity are also observed in tribal customs of North American Indians, as illustrated in these two references from Rosenblatt et al. (1976, 38):

> *A man in deep mourning painted his entire face black; in less extreme mourning he painted a black circle around each eye. . . . The custom of cutting the hair or wearing it unbraided, and of wearing old clothing was universally accepted.*
>
> Chippewa Customs, 1929

> *Very close kin were expected to show their sorrow at the death of a loved one not only by crying and wailing, but also by casting off their good clothes and donning old ones—robes, for instance, consisting of pieces of old discarded lodge covers . . . and by the cutting of hair.*
>
> *Close kin were also expected to go off into the hills, and fasting, crying aloud as they wandered about alone, and sleeping without shelter.*
>
> Regina Flannery, "The Gros Ventres of Montana"

Searching Themes as Depicted in Dreams

The searching, wandering theme is frequently depicted in the dreams of the survivor shortly after the child's death. Although I received numerous samples of such dreams, they are characteristic of the following example provided by Carol, a mother whose infant died in the twentieth week.

As with my analysand Sally, Carol's loss was made more difficult since her relationship with the child's father ended shortly after she learned she was pregnant. Although she was not married to the child's father, Carol resolved not to terminate the pregnancy, which eventually ended in a stillbirth. Two years after the stillborn death of her son, Carol wrote in the *Loving Arms Newsletter* (Nov. 1987):

Being a single parent who suffers a loss magnifies the word LONELY. *I didn't have a close person to turn to. To vent my feelings and lessen the loneliness, I joined a parents' support group. I'd often hear couples talk about relationship problems that occurred after their baby's death. Mostly, they described their grieving differences: She was up, he was down; she cried too much, he didn't cry at all. I recall wishing I had someone to cross swords with me. To escape from my loneliness, I imagined that my child's father felt the same way I did.*

Following the loss of her son, Carol had four dreams that were related by their similar searching themes.

Dream:

The dreams all started in a hospital after the baby was born. A nurse comes to my room to tell me I had a son but she didn't have him. She'd leave the room but never return. Then I'd get out of bed and search the hospital, asking everyone if they'd seen my baby. No one had. Some people helped me, others didn't. I'd never find him.

Searching dreams of this kind are common to the most intense period of grief, which occurs shortly after the death itself. Most parents who experienced dreams involving searching themes reported that such dreams stopped after three or four months. The cessation of the searching motif clearly corresponds to the survivor's acceptance of the reality of the loss—when they can no longer hope to have the actual child returned to them.

Later in her grieving process Carol dreamed that she was on her way to her first perinatal checkup. There she ran across her ex-boyfriend (the child's father) and talked about the baby with him. He was with his new girlfriend whom he assured that the baby was not his. She adds, "We didn't finish the conversation, just as we didn't finish it in real life."

As Carol had written in her article to *Loving Arms,* she had consciously tried to lessen her loneliness by imagining that the child's father felt the same way she did about the loss. Thus, this dream was disturbing to her, since in the dream she was confronted with a fact she was trying to avoid. Because of the dream, it is clear that Carol needed to come to terms with the harsh truth. She needed to face the betrayal that she had experienced with her ex-boyfriend. By becoming consciously aware of his indifference, she could then free herself from her tendency to overidealize him and thereby break her dependence on him. Her dependence was an impediment to her continued adjustment.

If her fantasy regarding her ex-boyfriend had continued unchecked, the searching motif that had been constellated by the death of their son would instead be misdirected toward the boyfriend. In either case, the resolution of her sorrow would be misperceived as residing within the literal act of regaining the lost person. Although she couldn't replace the lost child, Carol still hoped she could regain the lost relationship with her boyfriend. Despite her better judgment, for a time Carol felt almost compulsively concerned with her boyfriend: she kept hoping he would leave his new girlfriend; she would drive by his apartment hoping to meet him; or she would ask her friends for news regarding him. Although she felt foolish for such behavior, she was uanable to stop it. Ultimately Carol had to acknowledge the solitariness of her loss. It is this recognition that can ultimately transform loneliness into a more authentic sense of community. As Berry-Hillman explains it:

> We are indeed all, in part, orphans, and it is through the suffering of this archetypal fact of abandonment (and abandoning) that we can join together in community. This communal feeling, based on a recognition of our mutual aloneness and suffering, is a religious emotion, an existential reality, and a return to the world with a recognition that the world is all we have, and that maybe it is "good enough." (1985, 98–99)

The Color Black as Symbol of Shame

The use of the color black in Western mourning is derived from the color's symbolic association to Mother Nature. As Berry-Hillman explains:

> In early worship black animals were sacrificed to Gaia, Earth. The very word sacrifice means "to make sacred." Thus it is the "black" that is sacred to Gaia . . . Black, the dark, the depressed, grieving over losses, the inexplicable, the shadowy, the sinful. (1982, 6)

Therefore, embodied within this symbolic act of taking on blackness as an identity, the mourner enacts a ritualistic search for a relationship to Gaia, Mother Earth, whose dark side has reclaimed the mortal soul of the lost loved one. This metaphor is transfixed between the delicate psychological balance in the mourner of identifying with Gaia's black and devouring aspects, generated by a personal desire to remain in relation with the deceased child, and the act of sacrificing to Gaia something of one's individual identity, thus regaining the grace of Gaia's positive, life-giving aspect.

Also relevant to this discussion of blackness and its relationship to Gaia and death is, as Berry-Hillman explains, the etymological relationship between Mother and Matter. She states, "Mother and matter (*mater*) are cognates . . . Matter in this sense is itself a kind of chaos or, as Augustine describes it, an absence of light, a deprivation of being." She adds that "when we are close to our 'matter,' our lower substrates . . . we feel something unsettling, something inferior, chaotic, soiled" (1982, 3). In this existential experience of the "hour of lead," as Emily Dickinson describes it, we are in close connection to our dark shame, which is in itself a deeply rooted somatic experience. This is eloquently sung in this Navajo chant taken from Berry-Hillman's text:

> I am ashamed before earth;
> I am ashamed before heaven;
> I am ashamed before dawn;
> I am ashamed before twilight;
> I am ashamed before blue sky;
> I am ashamed before darkness;
> I am ashamed before sun;
> I am ashamed before that standing within me
>   which speaks with me.
> Some of these things are always looking at me.
> I am never out of sight.
> Therefore I must tell the truth.
> I hold my word tight to my breast.
>
> (1982, 5)

The depth of human shame, in the face of the divine, all knowing mysteries of life and death, as expressed in this Navajo chant is equivalent to the parents' personal experience of self-incrimination and blame. As has already been said, they feel deeply ashamed for their failure to nurture or protect the child from death. This shame, fundamental to this type of grief, is generally explained by psychologists as caused by the parents' perception of their inability to live up to the role expectation and functions assigned to parenthood in this culture. Although in part true, this level of understanding is insufficient and cannot fully comprehend the existential intensity of this deeply felt emotion. Throughout the literature on grief and mourning, authors mainly attribute *cause* to personalistic and societal factors. Implied within these societal interpretations is the assumption that the difficulties experienced by the mourner would, somehow, be ameliorated with a change in the culture. This ideological position is seen, for example, in Knapp's statement, "Survivors of child death have unique roles to fill because of the importance our society ascribes to the status of children" (1986, 12). The implication here, of course, is that it is society's ascription of value to children that causes the problem of loss, and, as such, society becomes a god-equivalent. No doubt patriarchal consciousness views its societal constructs as a dicty itself; but at its core, this attitude expresses the heroic inflation of modern man. Of concern here is how this modern perception of cause further moves us from a relatedness to the archetypally numinous. It is precisely this horrific struggle of personal shame that illustrates the weakness of such an approach. From my clinical and personal experiences with these parents, their shame is only partly diminished by an understanding of the societal factors contributing to it. Psychologically, there still remains a dark core, an almost impenetrable "sinfulness" or sense of inadequacy that prevails. This factor, in my opinion, accounts for the lifetime presence of shadow grief in many mothers. Their loving memories of the child are tainted with the affect of shame. It is uncanny that both Knapp and Peppers named it *shadow* grief. Unwittingly, they have captured its essence.

As Jung described his concept of shadow, it has at its core an archetypal "evil" as is, for example, symbolically represented by Satan. Thus, a conscious effort to integrate the shadow is ultimately a moral process. It requires of the person a psychological differentiation between his or her own personal responsibility and that "evil" which is, by its nature, greater than one can assume. Without such an archetypal perspective, parents struggling with their guilt and shame cannot fully liberate themselves from culpability.

In most instances, parents are not culpable in the death of their unborn child. However, even when some past action contributed to the death, the burden of guilt must be fairly and compassionately assessed. Such an example is seen with Sylvia, a young woman analysand who had consulted with me following the stillbirth of her child in the fifth month of pregnancy. The loss of the child was precipitated by an Rh sensitivity attributed to Sylvia's having shared a needle with a former partner during a period of cocaine addiction several years in the past. Since Sylvia was Rh positive, and her former partner was Rh negative, the exchange of blood which occurred with the sharing of needles resulted in the development of antibodies in Sylvia's blood stream. These antibodies then, several years later, attacked the fetus. Because of inadequate prenatal care, the situation became critical, and Sylvia lost the child in the fifth month of pregnancy.

Two months after their loss the couple came to see me. At the time,

Sylvia was suffering some depression, anxiety, inability to concentrate or sleep, she had night sweats and many disturbing nightmares. Although Sylvia assumed a tough and wizened persona, often using her sense of humor to conceal her vulnerability, it was clear nonetheless that she was deeply troubled by her culpability in losing this wanted child. She was frustrated by the fact that, despite her courageous and difficult recovery from addiction, she remained haunted by its effects. Following the loss of her child, she was informed that she would have only a one-in-eight chance of ever having a normal baby.

The death of the child reactivated in Sylvia her feelings of shame associated with her period of cocaine abuse, in addition to other feelings of inadequacy which Sylvia had suffered since early in life. She was the daughter of an abusive and alcholic father who frequently criticized and rejected her. Her mother, crippled by a stroke, was too disabled to offer her daughter much protection. In the short time I was able to work with Sylvia, I attempted to shift her identification of herself as the abusive "killing" parent (activated by the stillbirth) toward an understanding of herself also as victim. Sylvia acknowledged her culpability and accepted responsibility for it. However, given her vulnerable self-esteem, she was overly harsh on herself. Her dreams depicted her as under seige by nightmarish devils who tormented her. She remained in a heightened state of anticipation, ever anxious at work and at home. She was fearful of criticism and quick to accept blame for "making too much of my emotions" and "burdening my husband." It was clear that Sylvia could not compassionately acknowledge her mistakes but instead felt the need to ruthlessly punish herself just as she had previously been punished by her vindictive father.

The manifestations of the Search phase of grief, which I have described as including being unkempt, having sleepless nights, wearing of tattered clothing, being dirty, and so on, are embodied experiences of archetypal imagos that bring us deep into the realm of the personal body, or matter. It is common for parents who have lost a child at birth, produced a deformed or handicapped child, miscarried, or remained infertile, to unconsciously experience their bodies as *defectus incubus* (defective incubator), which then causes them to remain unwilling to have other children or, if they do, to live in dreadful fear of the outcome. This personal body-estrangement experienced as a defect also results in a psychological inability to enter into the body in other ways, such as through feeling and emotion or sexuality. Harriet Sarnoff Schiff states that "some studies estimate that as high as ninety percent of all bereaved couples are in serious marital difficulty within months of a dead child" (1978, 57). In part, the marital difficulty can be attributed to problems in sexuality between the couple. Fear of another conception, fear of intimacy or sexual pleasure can also be felt as a betrayal of the dead child. Within the somatic level of the unconscious, the experience of "letting go" sexually is analogous to the feeling of "letting go" of the desire to cling to the dead child. The associative similarities between sex and death are many. Swooning, for example, can refer either to swooning in grief (as Mary swooned at the foot of the cross) or to orgasmic passion. Similarly, passion, derived from the Latin *passus* means to endure or suffer. Referring to an intensity of feeling it therefore is also used to describe strong sexual desire.

Rage Aspects of the Search

Another form of passion experienced in mourning is the understandable feeling of rage that is evoked by the death of a child. Parents feel robbed of the promise of great joy and cannot help but seek to place the blame elsewhere. Anger then is directed toward the doctors, other parents of healthy children, spouses, other children, oneselves, and, of course, God. The projection of anger is, of course, a psychological defense, a warding off, and is normal to all grief. Knapp found, however, that parents whose children were murdered experienced the most pronounced rage, taking longer to resolve that anger than the anger experienced in other losses. This is explained by Knapp as resulting from the combination of several factors occurring simultaneously in the circumstances of a murdered child, which include: (1) suddenness of the loss; (2) violence; (3) intentionality of the murder; and (4) absence of choice or helplessness of the victim (1986, 86–87). The agony of living through such an event, which is reinacted incessantly in the survivor's mind, is not easy to comprehend for those who have not suffered it. For those parents, the murder constellates a strong urge for revenge— most strongly in fathers—which, if not openly discussed and confronted, can be acted out or misdirected within the family. Although usually a transitory state of identification with the masculine, archetypal paradigm of the vengeful God, its ultimate intent is a defense "against a force which seems chaotically overwhelming" (Eisendrath-Young 1984, 148).

Anger and rage can also be directed inward toward the self, as in depression or thoughts of suicide. When anger is directed toward the dead child itself, which most parents find disturbing, it can result in an unconscious need for self-punishment in order to expiate their perceived guilt. This theme is taken up in the Demeter-Persephone myth that Berry-Hillman, among others, discusses.

In this myth, Demeter, one of the twelve great Olympians and the goddess of agriculture, loses her daughter Persephone to Hades, the god of the underworld. Hades steals Persephone while she gathers flowers in a field. As the myth states:

> Bitter pain seized [Demeter's] heart, and she rent the covering upon her divine hair with her dear hands: her dark cloak she cast down from both her shoulders and sped, like a wild-bird, over the firm land and yielding sea, seeking her child. But no one would tell her the truth, neither god nor mortal man; and of the birds of omen none came with the news of her. Then for nine days queenly [Demeter] wandered over the earth . . . so grieved that she never tasted ambrosia.

> On the 10th day Hecate tells Demeter that she had heard the lost daughter's voice, and the two goddesses go to Helios, god of the sun, to ask of Persephone's whereabouts. Helios asks Demeter to cease her lament but, in response, "a grief yet more terrible and savage come into the heart of Demeter" and she wandered throughout the earth looking for her daughter. In despair . . . she caused a most dreadful and cruel year for mankind over the all-nourishing earth: The ground would not make the seed sprout, for rich-crowned Demeter kept it hid. . . . She would have destroyed the whole race of man with cruel famine . . . had not Zeus perceived and marked this in his heart. Zeus then sends Hermes to Hades to return Persephone to her mother. Although returned, Persephone must remain with Hades for one-third of each year. Nonetheless, Demeter rejoices and returns to earth its plentitude. (1980, 70–74)

Demeter's internalized, and thereby psychologically displaced, aggression is nonregenerative. Allowed to follow its own rageful course unimpeded by any external or internal restraints, such anger culminates in dire consequences for both the individual and those around them. As Berry-Hillman explains, "The depression of Demeter manifests itself with a certain dry asceticism. . . . But alongside this dryness she weeps with vain and insatiate anger" (1982, 22). The harmful consequence of Demeter's rage is clear in the following passage from the "Hymn to Demeter":

For she is thinking about/ the enormous act/ of wiping out/ that weak race/ of men/ who are born on earth/ concealing/ their seeds/ in the ground/and thus annihilating/ the honors/ of the gods . . . . (Ibid., 32).

The expression of anger in grief among mourners is a difficult issue faced by all societies. As Rosenblatt, Walsh, and Jackson found in their study of primitive cultures, the expression of anger must be contained by strict ritual, otherwise it erupts and becomes a greater risk to the group at large. The ritualized restriction employed by cultures included enforced periods of isolation, marking of the mourner, or projection of responsibility for the death onto an object or spirit (1976, 36–38).

Many couples have reported anger taking the form of blaming the spouse. Sometimes the blame was for the other's perceived failure to prevent the death. More often it is experienced as anger toward the spouse for failing to compassionately understand the other partner's grief. Many mourners, for example, have reported that they perceived their spouses as uncaring, projecting upon them all kinds of criticism and judgment beyond what they could possibly feel. During a couple's support group one woman said, "I just knew when he walked in the door and saw me still in my pajamas, unshowered and unkempt that he'd be mad at me for wallowing in my pain." In contrast, her husband explained that he generally felt helpless rather than mad. However, when his wife cast toward him her expectant glare, which seemed to say "you failed me by leaving me alone again" he would get defensive. "Within a few minutes we'd be fighting."

Weeping Aspects of the Search

Lastly, I would like to address that aspect of the Search which includes weeping. This phase of the discussion has been reserved to the end since with tears comes the promise of resolution. Crying is such an essential aspect of grief that mourning cannot be imagined without it. Therefore, the absence of crying is generally considered a strong indication of a psychological disturbance. For humans, crying is a fundamental manifestation of our need. As A.F. Shand describes it, it stems from "primitive roots" and has a "social value." The "cry of sorrow . . . tends to preserve the life of the young by bringing those watching over them to their assistance" (Bowlby 1980, 27). Similarly, Darwin states that "the muscle movements engaged and the expressions exhibited in anxiety, grief, and despair . . . are derived from an infant's screaming.

In all cases of distress . . . our brains tend to send an order to certain muscles to contract as if we are still infants on the point of screaming out" (*ibid.*, 25).

As any parent who has lost a child can affirm, crying or weeping is the most pronounced emotional experience in grief. Although at first, the tears appear to spring from a source of shock and pain, weeping's restorative value is, however, eventually felt. The healing function attributed to tears is seen in the many "miracles" within the Catholic faith of the weeping statues of Mary. Tears, like water, have a purifying function. Thus Eliade explains, "the waters symbolize the entire universe of the virtual; they are the *fons et origo* . . . they precede every form and sustain every creature " (as quoted in Warner 1976, 222).

In alchemy, water represents the stage of *liquefatio* which, when applied to the *prima materia*, begins the process of dissolution and a changing of the structure of matter. In this same way, the quality of tears shifts from an unrelenting emptying to accompanying tender and loving remembrances. The Archbishop of Syracuse—where a weeping plaque of Mary exists—rejoiced at the Virgin's weeping, and proclaimed, as described by Warner:

> *Mary has wept! Mary has wept! Weeping is fecund. There has never been a sterile tear. . . . And if Mary weeps beside the Cross of Jesus—I can tell you that her weeping was fertile and made her a mother.* (Warner 1976, 223)

Penetrating into the intense interiority of the dark experience of the Search, without undue censoring or ego prohibition, is an arduous and frightening task. Nonetheless, by cooperating as much as is humanly possible with the unfolding of the experience as itself, the intent of the Self can be made conscious. The ego's cooperation with this archetypal unfolding is in itself equivalent to assuming a religious attitude. The first dawning into conscious of the healing capacity of the Self is experienced in the fourth phase of this process, the Recovery.

Chapter 5

Archetypal Patterns of Mourning:
The Recovery

Do not return. If you can bear to, stay dead with the dead. The
dead have their own tasks. But help me, if you can without dis-
traction, as what is farthest sometimes helps: in me.
                    Rainer Maria Rilke, "Requiem," *Duino Elegies*

The psychological phase corresponding to the *recovery* is experienced
as a fundamental shift within the feeling of grief induced foremost by a
psychological loosening of the parental bond toward the *external* child
and the subsequent development of an inner relationship to the child's
image.

"Suffering," says Kübler-Ross, "has lost its meaning." The meaning
lost is, as Edinger explains, something that "affirms life" and "relates us
organically to life as a whole" (1972, 108). It is the outcome of the
psychological relationship to the symbolic life as opposed to an exclusively reductive "objective meaning." As Jung states:

> [Humans are] in need of a symbolic life. . . . But we have no symbolic
> life. . . . And, because we have no such thing, [we] can never step out of
> this mill—this awful grinding, banal life in which we are "nothing but."
> (1954)

Although the loss of any significant viable relation to symbol could,
perhaps, be tolerated within the course of everyday life, at times of
crisis its absence is profoundly felt. As Edinger explains: "To be able
to recognize the archetype, to see the symbolic image behind the symptom, immediately transforms the experience. It may be just as painful,

but now it has meaning" (1972, 116). Modern psychology, with its reductive and rationalistic approach, has reduced the symbolic to the secular. Within this psychological framework, "There can be no true symbols, only signs. . . . For those of this persuasion, religious symbolism is no more than evidence of ignorance and primitive superstition. . . . The symbolic per se is granted no substantive reality" (*ibid.*, 111). Freud's theory, predicated on the primacy of the ego, described the ego as engaged in a dance of supremacy with the unconscious, which he viewed as the repository of the instincts and ego-repudiated traits. "This concept," explains Edinger, "views the unconscious psyche as motivated only by the instincts [and] is basically anti-spiritual, anti-cultural, and destructive to the symbolic life" (*ibid.*, 114). Combined with his concept of the reality principle, Freud viewed mourning as a natural process that after a lapse will be overcome through the ego's *elevation* from the unconscious. The psychological task in mourning, then, is the turning away from the unconscious and its symbols, which is done at the behest of reality.

Reality, in Freud's theory, became the primary mediator, and, congruently, adjustment was its goal. As Freud stated, "No libido position is willingly abandoned and thus the bereaved may turn away from reality, through the medium of a hallucinatory wish-psychosis in order to maintain the relationship with the deceased." Ultimately, however, "deference to reality gains the day. The libido is eventually transferred to a new object, and the ego becomes free and uninhibited again." As stated earlier, Freud queried however, "why this process of carrying out the behest of reality bit by bit . . . should be so extraordinarily painful is not at all easy to explain in terms of mental economics" (Freud 1983, 165–66).

In contrast, Jung writes in "Adaptation, Individuation and Collectivity," that psychological adaptation consists of *two* equally essential processes, those of adaptation to outer conditions and adaptation to inner conditions. He elaborates that "by outer conditions are meant not only the conditions of the surrounding world, but also my conscious judgments, which I have formed of objective things" (1976, par. 1085). By inner conditions is meant "those facts or data which force themselves upon my inner perceptions from the unconscious, independently of my conscious judgments and sometimes even in opposition to it. Adaptation to inner conditions would thus be adaptation to the unconscious" (*ibid.*, par. 1086).

Before proceeding further, it is necessary to the discussion of the archetypal stage of recovery to elucidate the meaning of "image" as it is experienced within the psyche. This is essential to prevent later confusion between the actual child and his *image*, which in psyche's realm, is nonetheless real.

As an archetypal motif, recovery is variously enacted by the different goddesses. There is, for example, a bringing back to life of the son/lover, as with Isis; the eventual rejoining in Heaven, as with the Assumption of Mary; the sacrifice of the son/lover to the underworld, as with Innana; or a compromise with the Gods for the daughter's return, as with Demeter.

As enacted by the *human* counterpart, the recovery is, in contrast, an internal, psychologically differentiated embodiment of the *image* of the child within the consciousness of the parent. Simultaneously, there is an affectual altering in the experience of mourning that enables the grieved parent to psychologically *relate to this image*, and thereby manifest the parenthood he or she had otherwise been denied.

This psychological process is explained by Jung in his remark regarding the transformation of the libido:

> *If a man's libido goes to the unconscious, the less it goes to a human being; if it goes to a human being, the less it goes to the unconscious.* But *if it goes to a human being, and it is a true love, then it is the same as if the libido went directly to the unconscious, so very much is the person a* representative of the unconscious, *though only if this person is truly loved. Only then does love give him the quality of a* mediator, *which otherwise and in himself he would not possess.* (1969, par. 453)

As discussed by Corbin in his article on the *mundus imaginalis*, the modern mental association with the term "imaginary" is "equated with the unreal, with something that is outside the framework of being" (1972, 1). Corbin then proposes the use of the Latin term *mundus imaginalis* in reference to those psychological experiences of a metaphysical nature which give veracity to the experiences of dreams, symbolic rites, and, above all, spiritual meaning perceived in "imaginative information" (*ibid.*, 8–9). Through Persian and Gnostic texts, he illustrates how, once a spiritual journey has been completed, "the reality which has hitherto been an inner and hidden one turns out to envelop, surround, or contain that which at first was outer and visible. . . . Spiritual reality can therefore not be found 'in the where.' The 'where' is in it. In other words, spiritual reality itself is the 'where' of all things" (*ibid.*, 5). Imagination, or image, also contains this spiritual reality and is further equated with the Gnostic "subtle body" of soul and in the stage of recovery psychologically corresponds to *Impregnatio*, the birth of the homunculus in the alchemical transmutation of matter. Perceived as psychically real, the image of the dead child, once sufficiently differentiated from the *actual* child, then serves as "psychopomp," or mediating image, to the world of the unconscious. The fructifying capacity of the mediated image is, for example, acknowledged in the shamanistic death rituals of the Mayanian culture. The souls of the dead are seen as ultimately reborn into the tribe, thereby guaranteeing fertility in the fields and the herds. In the words of von Franz, "The goal is not to float away into a divine spiritual Beyond, but to increase the working of fertility in this life" (1986, 5). In this regard, primitive humans had one distinct advantage over their modern counterparts: They were able to maintain the connection to their lost loved ones through the spiritual and cultural recognition of their loved ones' regenerative capacity. We can only speculate what effect this had on their grief: Did they, forced by the primitive conditions of their lives, become accustomed to death and therefore grieve less long or less profoundly than we? Or, if there was any diminution in sorrow, would it better be attributed to the enduring nature of the relationship that their culture provided them? As Rosenblatt, Walsh, and Jackson found in their cross-cultural studies, ghost cognitions appear fundamentally human and "arise preponderantly out of the *residue of close relationships*" (1976, 55).

In the Beatitudes it is said, "Blessed are those who mourn, for they shall be comforted." In Edinger's interpretation of this, he concludes that "mourning is caused by the loss of a love object who was carrying an important projected value. In order to withdraw projections and assimilate their contents into one's own personality it is necessary to experience the loss as a prelude to rediscovering the content or value within. Therefore, mourners are involved in a growth process" (1972, 136). Thus mourning, from this perspective, is, as Asclepius named it, the "divine affliction."

I do not wish, however, to create through the preceding remarks the idea that mourning for a deceased child is confined only to the child's projected value. In this way, as Satinover puts it, the search for meaning can be viewed as a "defense against the pain of object loss" (1985, 57). Certainly the loss of an older child is genuinely grieved: His or her unique personality, the manner of speech, the sense of charm and humor, or the helpless purity of the child are all personal attributes that the parent cannot help but miss. In infant or perinatal losses, however, the tragedy of death has occurred before the infant's personality has emerged, therefore, the parental attachments are more clearly based on the meaning they attributed to the child and the future family life.

Dreaming of the Lost Child

Dream images, combined with the intense feelings they may elicit, often disturb one's wakeful state. In times of crisis, dreams have just such an effect. Mourners often report that their dreams take up the subject of their loss and, in doing so, produce intensified feelings of longing, sadness, helplessness, and guilt, or, paradoxically, great peace and acceptance.

As a psychoanalyst, I, of course, regard dreams as meaningful. Although difficult to understand, the meaning of a dream is made more comprehensible through an understanding of the dreamer's circumstances as well as the symbolic language of the unconscious. In general, dreams tend to compensate one's conscious attitude by including neglected or repressed thoughts and feelings, to expand the depth of one's conscious personality, and to restore psychological equilibrium.

Dreams enhance the natural resolution of mourning by attempting to make conscious both the actual and the symbolic influence that the deceased had on the survivor's life. The actual influence includes, for example, the roles and functions that the deceased would have occupied, the companionship that that person might have offered, and the ways in which that life would have enriched the survivor. The symbolic influence is derived more from the meaning we attach to the relationship, as when I, by parenting a healthy child, become a nurturing, supportive person. Dreams are a primary means of apprehending the less obvious symbolic meaning of the relationship, which must be realized for mourning to become complete.

Dreams also enhance the natural progression of mourning by presenting to the dreamers a candid depiction of the depth of their emotional attachment to the deceased. Although such knowledge may cause one to feel more acutely the pain of the separation, such images compensate for the conscious tendency to minimize the sorrow. Such psychological frankness is necessary in order to fully comprehend the nature of the loss.

Strange as it may seem, the continuity of the relationship between the deceased and the survivor is preserved by the dreams. This continuity enables the bereaved to accept the finality of the loss, understand the uniquely personal nature of the loss, and comprehend the meaning of the loss. Comprehension is accomplished within a gradually evolving process of reintegration.

Dream images also amplify otherwise unconscious ideas and feelings the survivor holds toward the deceased. In circumstances of miscarriage, neonatal death, or stillbirth, dream images of the child help give reality to the child, which then enables the parent to consciously acknowledge the loss and openly mourn. Without such conscious recognition, the unrecognized grief may manifest itself in such pathological conditions as displacing onto other surviving children feelings about the deceased child.

Dreams help survivors' self-esteem by enabling dreams to become less identified with the negative influences of the loss. This is an example of the compensatory nature of dreams. As previously stated, a mother who has suffered a childbearing loss often feels responsible for the death and, consequently, is fearful of attempting another pregnancy. She may then perhaps dream that the child who died is safely nestled in the lap of a loving god or that she is the mother of a dozen healthy children. Each dream provides the dreamer with the possibility of resolving the guilty feelings.

Whether one understands the meaning of a dream, the dream still influences the dreamer. Often one mistakenly believes that psychological gains have been made through conscious effort. In fact, however, the gains may have been already initiated by an earlier dream. If one attempts to understand the meaning of dreams, the process of resolving grief is generally enhanced. The frequency of these kinds of dreams may diminish in time; yet it is not unusual to dream of the lost child for a lifetime. In many instances the dream image of the child may grow just as an actual child ages in life. In this sense, one remains forever a parent to the deceased child and, through the psychological reality of this intrapsychic relationship, the parent is able to express the love that the death had thwarted.

This theme is addressed in the dream provided by Ronda, whose almost full-term son, Adam, was killed in a car accident late in Ronda's pregnancy. She survived her injuries but lost the baby. She dreamed:

I am living in an unfamiliar house with two of my sisters and their children. There is a lot of activity going on—typical child-rearing kinds of activity—but I am sitting apart. I walk into a bedroom in the back of the house and there is Adam. He is about one year old and he seems to recognize me. I cannot believe my eyes, but I pick him up and carry him to the living room. My sisters seem to take it right in stride, as if Adam had been in the room all along—as if he was never dead. There is some talk about going and leaving the children with a baby sitter. I feel reluctant to go and leave Adam. I am afraid that if I come back, he will be gone. I hold him on my lap in a rocking chair. I put my lips on his head and rock him.

Ronda had this dream early in the second year after Adam's death. The age of the dream-image Adam corresponded closely to what his actual age would have been. The dream depicts Ronda as still being psychologically unable to engage herself fully in child-rearing activities. Given her loss, it is understandable that such activities would constellate in her feelings of grief toward both her lost child and the motherhood that was denied her in the death of her child.

At this point in her life, the dream suggests that Ronda needs to be reminded of her own capacity to nurture and of her identity as a mother. In the dream Ronda is reminded that she too *is* a mother and, if she can accept the inner reality of her motherhood, she need not fear losing it again. In the dream, she rocks the baby and holds him, while tenderly kissing the son whose image in the unconscious has grown from an infant to a one year old. This ever-changing development of the image of the child underscores the continuing evolution of the parent-child relationship within the psyche of the dreamer.

The capacity of the psyche to keep track of time and maintain the congruence of imagery with external events is also depicted in a dream provided by my analysand Susan. When she was in her early twenties, Susan had surrendered a child to adoption. This event had been a difficult period in her life and continued to cause her some persisting feelings of shame and guilt. Now 37, she had entered analysis in order to better understand her loss and the feelings of shame and inadequacy that the adoption had constellated.

In the course of the analysis, Susan had contacted the adoption agency, had given them her current address, and had confessed her illegitimate pregnancy to her only remaining relative, a sister. For over 16 years this event had remained a secret to everyone but her present husband. She was now determined to make a place in her life for her son, should he ever decide to try to find her. Six months into the analysis she dreamed:

> I am in a store in a small town. I think I am traveling or have moved here. I am with my son. He is 16 or 17 years old, handsome, blond-haired but slightly retarded. I live alone here with my son. Some men in the store comment on what a nice young man I have with me. One man offers to help my son put two pieces of something together. My son is having a problem doing it alone. Then my son picks out a realistic stuffed toy dog, like Lassie, which I buy for him. It is a poignant and joyfully sad dream. I feel a great sense of peace and love. It was so wonderful to see my son again.

Susan was deeply moved by this dream. She felt that the image of her son as slightly retarded reflected the shame she felt about his illegitimacy. Because of the combined circumstance of his illegitimacy and her decision to surrender him for adoption, she could not openly acknowledge her maternal love for him. Archetypally, the image of the son as retarded or moronic is associated with the archetype of the fool, or the clown. As Frazer amplifies it, the fool, or clown, played the part of the "scapegoat" in ritual sacrifice (1922, 767). The scapegoat was the sacrificial goat of the Old Testament over whose head Aaron confessed all the sins of the children of Israel. The goat was then sent into the wilderness, symbolically bearing their sins until the Day of Atonement.

Thus the image of the retarded son in Susan's dream represents on the subjective level the rejected element in Susan's personality as well as the actual son she was forced to reject. In the dream, she is reunited with her son, who then receives help from another in putting "two pieces of something together." Susan associated this image with the splitting effect her illegitimate pregnancy had had on her life. Quite simply, her life had been split in two, separated by a secret she had been forced to keep. With the help of her emerging need to reunite these two halves of her life (as imaged in the helpful male dream figure), Susan found the courage to face her shame. In response to the final image of the dream, Susan stated, "I was never able to give my son anything. It felt wonderful in the dream to be able to give him the toy of his choosing. It is something all mothers want to do."

Jung states that the process of healing can take place only "when the imago that mirrored itself in the object is restored, together with its meaning, to the subject. This restoration is achieved through the conscious recognition of the projected content, that is, by acknowledging the 'symbolic' value of the object" (1969a, par. 507).

In childbearing loss, the restoration of the projected contents back into the conscious awareness of the parent is observed in a change of character of the "imaged" child in dreams, waking visualizations, synchronistic events, or a shift within the affectual realm of the survivor. According to von Franz (1986) certain dreams exist in which the deceased's appearance or manner is particularly striking to the dreamer. In some inexplicable way, this image stands apart from other images of the deceased as seen in past dreams by its acuity and intensity. Von Franz comments on Jung's extraordinary capacity to intuitively interpret these dreams on the "objective" level rather than the "subjective," which would attribute its symbolic content to aspects of the dreamer's own psyche. Von Franz adds, "One can 'feel' whether the figure of the dead person in a dream is being used as a symbol for some inner reality or whether it 'really' represents the dead" (1986, xv).

I have approached such dreams from the following perspective. In the first place, the imagistic difference from other representations of the deceased is due to its direct derivation from the Self, which accounts for its numinosity. In the second place, these acute dream images of the deceased are representations that are stripped of the residual distortions of projection by the dreamer and thus represent the deceased in a more "pure" or less polluted way. If this fact is consciously comprehended by the dreamer, it results in a corresponding freeing of the bond to the actual dead child.

Let me illustrate through an example from my practice, dealing, however, with the loss of a husband rather than a child. A woman in her mid-30s entered analysis to enable her to cope better with the sudden death of her husband in a tragic, work-related accident. Her mourning was complicated by the fact that she was, at the time of his death, seven months pregnant. She had many dreams in which her husband Charlie appeared. Most of the dreams had to do with recalling scenes from the hospital as he lay brain-dead and comatose. Other dreams, which could be seen as subjective in nature, dealt with personal aspects of Charlie and her feelings toward these personal aspects. After the birth of her son, and five months following her husband's death, she came to an analytical session quite agitated. Her dreams of Charlie had progressively diminished, but she had now had a very vivid dream in which Charlie was simply standing before her, just as he was before the accident, relaxed, but strangely "different." The dreamer could not explain how he was different, "he just was." She had awakened from this dream very disturbed. In the session she became quite distressed and kept saying, "That was Charlie . . . that was Charlie." What she later was able to realize through discussing this dream was that she "didn't really know him"; that is, she had not experienced his essence or "soul" owing to her own rather narcissistic nature. This image of the dead husband was, as Corbin would describe it, "the almond that is concealed by the shell" (1972, 5), also Gnostically referred to as the "subtle body" of image.

Similarly, the vivid dream of the woman who found her baby snuggled in the nest of the warm cave of the Great Mother is another example of the numinous dream that further freed the dreamer from the possessive bonds to the dead child.

This "subtle body" of image is also associated with the "body of the resurrection," which brings me back to the mythical parallels to the stage of recovery. As enacted in the goddess myths, the goddess herself, imbued with life-giving power, literally resurrected the son or daughter through some act of her own or in collaboration with other deities. Once the child was reborn, the goddess was released from her grief. Mary, the mother of God, however, being first a mortal woman, did not possess this same literal regenerative capacity as, for example, Isis possessed. Instead, Mary, like all parents who have lost a child, can only stand in grief at the foot of the cross. Her only comfort is in her knowledge, or "image," of Christ's eternal resurrection. From this perspective, Mary's drama is a striking parallel to the circumstances of all bereaved parents. As an eternal image of a mother who enacts the conception and birth, shows a loving but nonpossessive motherhood, and grieves at the death of her son, Mary amplifies the psychological meaning of Eros.

Also essential to the recovery stage of this paradigm is the psychological development of an Eros relationship with the deceased child. Eros, as von Franz explains, is "a relatedness which proceeds, not from the ego but from a transcendental inner center, the Self." Within the matrix of the relationship between the surviving parent and the deceased child, the parental longing for the child potentially evolves into an Eros-love which recognizes the deceased child as separate from the parental projections that were previously attached to it. This psychological differentiation then frees the projected content to be reintegrated into the parent, and concurrently, the child is revealed as an autonomous entity in its own right. The reintegration of the projected, subjective content occurs with the development of the corresponding "imaginal" child which then acts as psychopomp between the conscious and unconscious realms. As von Franz explains it, however, before such reintegration occurs, the projections will always "appear physically because it forces the subject into its own form" (1980, 105). Thus, the transcendent image first takes its form in the image of the actual child. Only later does the image of the actual child differentiate itself from the imaginal and mediating image, which, by virtue of its twin structure, reveals its synthesizing function, or the *hieros gamos* (sacred union) between heaven and earth.

Thus, Eros and its behavioral expression, relatedness, express the social function of the Self, also known as reciprocal individuation.

As Whitmont clarifies it:

> *Relatedness is not to be confused with the* longing *of personal involvement and empathetic identification. . . . Such involvement does not neces-*

sarily constitute relatedness without *a corresponding awareness of the
separate identity of each partner. . . . Relatedness involves a willingness
and ability to perceive and appreciate the other just as he or she is while
maintaining one's own genuine position.* (1984, 131)

In conclusion, the psychological experience of recovery within this
archetypal paradigm proceeds through an inner distinction between the
actual child and its image. Once this inner image is accepted as having a
reality of its own, it can then serve as a mediator to the unconscious of
the survivor. In child—and certainly in infant—death, the maintenance
of inner relationship between parent and child augments the healing
process by the loosening of the bonds with the actual dead child while
still preserving the parent's spiritual connection to him or her. In the
archetypal realm this incorruptibility of the spiritual connection is expressed as a literal recovery of the lost child. The human counterpart,
however, is "imaginal." Within the experience of the mourning parent,
this recovery of the spiritual connection results in a deepening of the
personality, an experiential encounter with the Self, which transcends
the needs or wants of the ego. Von Franz describes this recovery of the
spiritual connection as leading to "a change of character . . . through
which the entire personality is renewed and altered in such a way that it
is irreversible . . . and is for the most part experienced as coming from
within" (1980, 161). This revitalization is expressed in the following
poem from the Minnesota SIDS Newsletter, Vol. 4, No. 3, Dec. 1983:

Healing

I feel my body
come alive
again.
Out of the shadows
it rises.
Senses quicken
and once more
I know
joy.
Many times
did I despair
would I forever
be dead?
So long
did I hunger
after life
but to no avail.

Yet one day
slowly
did I begin
to waken.

And now
more and more
the momentum gathers.
I heal
I integrate
I become
I live
Thank God
I live.

— Candy McLaughlin

Chapter 6

Archetypal Patterns of Mourning: Rebirth, the Resolution of Mourning, and the Expansion of Consciousness

How we squander our hours of pain,
how we gaze beyond them into the bitter duration
to see if they have an end. Though
they are really our
winter-enduring foliage, our
dark evergreen,
one season in our inner year—
not only a season in time—
but are place and settlement
foundation and soil and home.

But if the endlessly dead awakened a symbol in us,
perhaps they would point to the catkins hanging from the bare
branches of the hazel-trees, or
would evoke the raindrops that fall onto the dark earth in springtime.

And we, who have always thought
of happiness as rising, would feel
the emotion that almost overwhelms us
whenever a happy thing falls.
                    —Rainer Maria Rilke, "The Tenth Elegy"

> Some people
> come into our lives
> and quickly go.
>
> Some stay for awhile
> and leave footprints on our hearts,
> and we are never,
> ever the same.
>   *Flavia*

A Buddhist poem from the Samyutta Nikaya, entitled "Kisagotami" and more popularly known as "The Mustard Seed Medicine," details the story of a grieving mother who wanders throughout her village carrying the corpse of her dead son in her arms. Beseechingly, she seeks the help of anyone who might revive him; but in her madness, she was rebuked by all except for one wise man who tells her to seek the wisdom of the Buddha. Later, upon finding the Buddha, Kisagotami approaches, asking him to bring her son's youthful body back to life. The Buddha instructs her to "go, enter the town, and at any house where yet no man hath died, thence bring a little mustard seed." Eagerly she searches several houses but then realizes what the Buddha had wished to have her learn. She then laid the corpse of her son in the charnel field and said:

> No village law is this, no city law,
> No law for this clan, or for that alone,
> For the whole world—ay, and the gods in heaven—
> This is the Law: ALL IS IMPERMANENT!

When Kisagotami returns to the Buddha he tells her:

> To him whose heart on children and on goods
> is centered, cleaving to them in his thoughts,
> Death cometh like a great flood in the night,
> Bearing away the village in its sleep.
> (Rhys-Davies 1932)

In her poem from the Bhikkuni Samyutta, Kisagotami later speaks with Mara, the incarnation of death, saying:

> I have finished with the death of my child,
> and men belong to that past.
> I don't grieve,
> I don't cry,
> *I am not afraid of you my friend.*

> Everywhere the love of pleasure is destroyed,
> and the great dark is torn apart,
> *and death*
> *you are destroyed yourself.*

The preceding psalm reflects the uniquely Buddhist conception of the nature of pleasure (joy) and suffering. The pleasure of possessing a child, within an unenlightened condition, is beneath the highest level of Buddhist happiness (*cetasika sukha*) since it is not yet free of selfish individual interest and limitation. Similarly, believing that the child's life belongs to the parent is one of the many illusions (*moha*) of man. Suffering (*domanassa*), then, is "nothing but hampered will, fighting in vain against obstacles it has created by its own tendency of separation and limitation" (Conze 1963).

In another psalm, the Buddha consoles the weeping mother Paracara, acknowledging that he too had shed tears because of the death of children. Yet the Buddha's grief had occurred within the unending round of life and death, which is "more abundant than the waters of the ocean." Patacara, the founder of the Order of Nuns (Bhikkunis), then advises her followers, 500 bereaved mothers:

> Why mourning then for him who came to thee,
> Lamenting, through thy tears, "My son! My son!"
>
> Seeing thou knowest not the way he came,
> Nor yet the manner of his leaving thee?
> Weep not, for such is here the life of man.
> Unask'd he came, unbidden went he hence.
> Lo! ask thyself again whence came thy son
> to bide on earth this little breathing space?
> By one way come and by another gone,
> As man to die, and pass to other births —
> So hither and so hence — why would ye weep?
> (Rhys-Davies 1932)

As illustrated by these Buddhist psalms, these grieving mothers were redeemed from their personal grief when they were able to disidentify from the child as "object" and thereby separate from their possessive or egoistic motherhood. Their relationship with the child remained eternal, however, evolving into a spiritual relationship with the child as "image." Released from the illusions (*moha* or *maya*) of mortal limitation, the mother was spiritually reunited with her "imaged" child whose soul had been reborn into the Great Round of Immortality, and the sanctity of the relationship was preserved. Similarly, as Esther Harding clarifies it, a mother must eventually

> *differentiate herself, and her egoistic desires, from her own offspring.*
> *If she becomes identified to the child, her personal satisfaction is found*

through seeking his good. Instead of now seeking her own way, her own advance in open egotism . . . she seeks the good of the child. She does not realize that this apparent altruism is in reality a concealed egotism. (1971, 194)

Ultimately, this psychological condition denies the child the opportunity to live his or her own life and death; the child's life instead becomes an extension, or narcissistic reflection, of the parent's need. This theme is illustrated in the myth of Demeter who attempts to offer Demophoon, the mortal son of Metaneira, the immortality of the gods. Paraphrasing from the Homeric Hymn to Demeter (Boer 1979), Metaneira had observed "the great marvel of [how] their son throve in Demeter's care. He was fair as one of the Gods." Nonetheless, when Metaneira witnessed Demeter burning the child with the flames of immortality, she intervened. Metaneira laments, "Demophoon, my son, the stranger lets thee waste in the great fire, and me she plunges into bereavement." Because of Metaneira's interference, her son was denied immortality. The greater good of the child was sacrificed to Metaneira's desire to protect him and thereby maintain her status of mother.

This same theme can be observed in the short Grimms' fairy tale entitled "The Aged Mother." The tale is as follows:

In a large town there was an old woman who sat in the evening alone in her room thinking how she had lost first her husband, then both her children, then one by one all her relatives, and at length, that very day, her last friend, and now she was quite alone and desolate. She was very sad at heart, and heaviest of all her losses to her was that of her sons; and in her pain she blamed God for it. She was still sitting lost in thought, when all at once she heard the bells ringing for early prayer. She was surprised that she had thus in her sorrow watched through the whole night, and lighted her lantern and went to church. It was already lighted up when she arrived, but not as it usually was with wax candles, but with a dim light. It was also crowded already with people, and all the seats were filled; and when the old woman got to her usual place it also was not empty, but the whole bench was entirely full. And when she looked at the people, they were none other than her dead relatives who were sitting there in their old-fashioned garments, but with pale faces. They neither spoke nor sang; but a soft humming and whispering was heard all over the church. Then an aunt of hers stood up, stepped forward, and said to the poor old woman: "Look there beside the altar, and you will see your sons." The old woman looked there, and saw her two children, one hanging on the gallows, the other bound to the wheel. Then said the aunt, "Behold, so would it have been with them if they had lived, and if the good God had not taken them to himself when they were innocent children." The old woman went trembling home, and on her knees thanked God for having dealt with her more kindly than she had been able to understand, and on the third day she lay down and died. (Grimm 1975, 826–27)

Thus, this mother, like her Greek predecessor Metaneira, would have unwittingly caused greater suffering for her sons had her motherly desire for their survival prevailed. This problem was resolved, however, by the occurrence of a synchronistic event, the ringing of the church bells, which then sent the grieving mother to mass. Within the vessel of her religious belief, she then learns what her motherly desire could not otherwise comprehend. Having understood the limiting nature of her longing, her grief is lifted and thus she is able to pass from life without regret. On the third day she laid down and died. The occurrence of such synchronistic events within the time-space intersection between life and death is commented on by von Franz. In *On Dreams and Death* she speculates: "There occurs at death perhaps a gradual liberation from the bonds of space-time, and seen thus it would not be surprising that it is especially in the vicinity of place where death has occurred that synchronistic phenomena occur most frequently" (1986, 154). In this folktale, the church bells symbolize the dawning of awareness that eventually liberates us from our narrow, egoistic concerns.

Within the Christian tradition, the transformation of rebirth occurs on a symbolic level (unlike its Buddhist counterpart which recognizes a literal rebirth through reincarnation). Within this doctrine, Christ's agony on the cross serves as a powerful symbol for the human encounter with one's own inevitable death. Mary, on the other hand, more closely parallels the experience of mourning within the survivor, and particularly mourning within the matrix of the parent-child relationship.

Mythologically, Mary is a syncretic link to the feminine goddesses before her. Aspects of Mary are foreshadowed in such ancient goddesses as Isis, Cybele, and Demeter. However, fundamental to apprehending her unique role in the theological evolution of humankind and her relevance to the topic of mourning is the recognition that Mary was a human woman. Thus, she is similar to Job, who, according to Jung, also experienced the dual nature of God. As Stein explains it, Jung's

Answer to Job conveyed to the Christian doctrine that its "transformation must result in a decisive inclusion of the 'natural man' who values knowledge and experience above faith and belief" (1985, 168). Similarly, Mary's story is based on the experience of the duality of the Godhead and embodies the full-life drama that begins with conception and ends with sacrifice. As such, it parallels the human experience of birth and death. Mary, then, is the quintessential symbol for human grief at the death of a child.

Like Job, Mary experienced the bounty of the Godhead as manifested through the Immaculate Conception. Foremost a mortal woman, Mary did not conceive the divine child herself, but is instead the "vessel" which the Holy Ghost impregnates. The Apostles' Creed, according to Warner, "clearly expresses the idea that the Holy Spirit carried the whole child into Mary's womb to be nourished there, rather than quickening it to life. The Holy Ghost, like a mother, conceived the child and then took possession of Mary until the day of the child's birth" (1976, 38). This relationship is also implied by the term "overshadowing" used to describe the predominant role of the Holy Spirit in the Annunciation. Mary's chosen role in the divine plan provided her with the experience of the fructifying capacity of God, experienced psychologically as an encounter with the Self. Thus, she responds in Luke 1:46–49:

> *And Mary said, "My soul magnifies the Lord, and my spirit rejoices in God my savior, for he has regarded the low estate of his handmaiden. For behold, henceforth all generations will call me blessed. . . ."*

Conversely, as the Mother of Sorrows, Mary suffered the dark side of God as she stood witness to the crucifixion of her only child at the foot of the cross. Behind the human mother stands the Mother of Life aspect of the primordial goddess. As a human, grieving mother, however, she is not equivalent to the goddess or she would have interceded on her son's behalf, as did her feminine predecessors. The cross on which her son is crucified symbolizes the Mother of Death aspect of this same primordial goddess. As Jung described it, the association of the cross with the dark aspect of the primordial feminine is revealed by the naming of the stakes upon which the ancient Greeks were executed "hecate" (1956, 271 n.155). In an Old English lament to which Jung refers, Mary accuses the cross of being a false tree that unjustly destroyed "the pure fruit of her body, with the poisonous draught of death, which was meant for the guilty descendants of the sinner Adam. Her Son was not to blame for their guilt." Mary laments:

Tree unkind thou shalt be known,
my son's stepmother I call thee:
Cross, thou holdest him so high in height,
my fruit's feet I may not kiss;
Cross, I find thou art my foe,
thou bearest my bird, beaten blue.

The Cross answers:

Lady, to thee I owe honor,
thy bright palms now I bear;
thy fruit flourisheth for me in blood colour . . .
that blossom bloomed up in thy bower.
And not for thee alone,
but to win all this world.

Jung then concludes, "Thus the Mother of Death joins the Mother of
Life lamenting the dying god, and as an outward token of their union,
Mary kisses the cross and is reconciled" (*ibid.*, par. 415). More accurately, however, this lament is made not by the Mother of Life herself
but by the human figure of Mary. It is a mere woman who cannot kiss
the feet of her son which are held above her reach. At this juncture, her
grief has not yet been transformed; this occurs later, in the third stanza,
when Mary comprehends the meaning behind her son's death and her
personal loss.

Thou art crowned Heaven's Queen
through the burden thou barest.
I am a Relic that shineth bright;
men desire to know where I am.

With this revelation, Mary then becomes the Queen of Heaven through
the burden she bears.

The importance of this distinction is essential to a sufficiently differentiated perception of the Christian figure of Mary. With this distinction the archetypal image is also brought into the realm of human experience and consciousness.

Mary, as portrayed by the Roman Catholic faith, has been tradition-
ally viewed as a symbolic equivalent to the Mother of Life, her origin
then extending back to the primordial Mother Goddess herself. The
Catholic Church's desire to resolve the problems posed by acknowledging her Assumption justified Mary's preordained divinity by the
New Testament vision of the Apocalypse in Revelation 12:1. "And a

great portent appeared in heaven, a woman clothed with the sun, and the Moon under her feet, and on her head a crown of twelve stars. . . ." At this level of symbolic representation, however, the archetypal image must, by its nature, contain the dual aspects of its paradoxical polarity. However, Mary the Mother of God is nowhere represented in Christian doctrine as a dark and terrible goddess. Instead, in service to the patriarchal intentions of the Church fathers, Mary, as symbol, became one-sidedly pure, which further contributed to her estrangement from the faithful, who could not emulate her purity within the "sinful" human condition of mankind. This estrangement was further aggravated by the Doctrines of the Immaculate Conception and the Assumption, which were predicated on the literal incorruptibility of her flesh and her exception from the stain of sin. Mary's viability as a symbol was thereby diminished and she instead became associated with a devotion that was too passive and yielding, a selflessness that was shapeless, and a purity that was too one-sidedly good. Furthermore, her now-purified image was contaminated by a passivity that bordered on indifference to the son's suffering. This resulted in the compensatory dramatization of her depth of sorrow as seen in the artistic depictions of her from the end of the eleventh century on (Warner 1976).

If, however, her humanness remains the central focus of her drama, her relevance to human life—and secondarily this book—is better apprehended. Like Job, she was the most pure of her fellow mortals. As Caelius Sedulius wrote:

> She . . . had no peer
> Either in our first mother (Eve) or in all women
> Who were to come. But alone of all her sex
> She pleased the Lord.
> (As quoted in Warner 1976, xvii)

As the chosen one, Mary then experienced the dual aspects of the divinity who remained elevated in the heavens above her. Ultimately, her task was to apprehend the meaning of the divine plan and throughout its fateful unfolding cooperate with its design. For Mary, this task was accomplished within the body of her love, or Eros; for Job the questioning of faith was within the realm of Logos. Thus, Mary "kept all these things, pondering them in her heart" (Matt. 2:19). And it is in her heart that she is so deeply wounded, as presaged by Simeon's prophecy on the eighth day following her son's birth: "And a sword will pierce through your own soul also" (Luke 2:35).

The unfolding of Mary's drama closely parallels the experience of other parents who have lost their children. The "divine child" is born within the mystery of birth. Like Mary, burdened by the foreknowledge of Christ's future agony on the cross because of Simeon's prophecy, parents whose children die at birth also encounter the tragic convergence of birth and death consolidated into a single moment. With the child's death, the bereaved parents' sorrow can only be released by finding a meaning for their loss. As Meier points out, "Jung does not mean [only] the healing of symptoms. He had in mind the goal of leading the patient to understanding the meaning of life, his suffering, of his being what he is. With this insight would come a religious attitude, not merely a remission, but a real cure, which could be called a transformation" (1967, 128). The Christian figure of Mary symbolizes the receptive attitude that awaits apprehension of the divine plan. Mary is not only a vessel by virtue of the incarnation of Christ, but she is also a vessel to the meaning of the loss. Like the ancient Greek who entered the *temenos*, Mary awaits the dream that will transform her sorrow. Mary teaches us the sanctity of life through her devotion to the individuation of the child. As Mother of Sorrow, she enacts the depth of human attachment as she holds the broken body of her son. Her grief is ultimately eased by her knowledge of her eternal relationship with him. With her Assumption into heaven, the transformative potential of sorrow is vividly depicted.

As Jung explained, the Assumption was of considerable importance:

> The dogmatization of the Assumptio Mariae *points to the hieros gamos in the pleroma, and this in turn implies . . . the future birth of the divine child . . . The metaphysical process is known to the psychology of the unconscious as the individuation process.* (1969c, pars. 46–48)

The Assumption is therefore the religious symbol for the transformation of sorrow within the human personality. The veracity of this image is made more relevant to the bereaved parent by virtue of Mary's humanness.

As outlined in the preceding chapter, the Recovery stage of the archetypal paradigm of mourning evolves psychologically through the development of a transcendent "image" of the child which, when sufficiently differentiated from the actual child, serves as a mediator between the conscious and unconscious realms within the bereaved's psyche. This transcendent image of the child is derived from the regulatory function of the Self, which accounts for the "numinous" quality given to the image. This natural process of image formation is illustrated in the following poem, written by a bereaved mother, entitled "The

Baby Has Died" (reprinted from *Feelings*, Cleveland Regional Perinatal Network). The first several stanzas deal with the mother's shock at the stillborn death and the period of grief that followed.

The Baby Has Died

"The baby has died."

The words no one can say.
Half-truths. Turning away. Avoiding eyes.
And pain becomes so powerful
That it pushes everything else far away.
So far away.

Were there ever good feelings?
Where is joy? Eager anticipation? Smiles?
Excitement? Pleasure? Most of all . . .
Where is love?
You feel nothing but pain.

Pain does go away. It uses itself up.
After its harsh, tormenting, and constant
Battering of self and soul,
Pain slowly stops. With cost, of course.
For feeling always costs.

And emptiness remains.
Sometimes the pain returns as part of the price of life.
But never with such intensity.
The memories of pain begin,
Yet are less intense.

Within the emptiness
The soul feels a different kind of loss
Before beginning its long task of repair and loneliness.
It seeks to find some warmth
Where harsh and constant pain once lived.
For emptiness is cold.

Yet life with its strong pull to keep on living
In the middle of wanting to die
Keeps the soul alive.
Urges the spirit to heal.
Tries to make sense out of nonsense;
Peace out of pain; and love out of loss.

Somehow the memories grow from pain
Into pictures of pretending

How this little life would have grown.
And become. And shared. And laughed. And cried.
And been a part of you.
Rather than apart from you.

The memory picture grows with time.
It begins to have a sense of comfort.
A sense of love. A sense of peace.
The emptiness of soul and the loneliness of self
Are lessened by a sense of warmth and love
That conquers the sometimes returning pain and sadness.

Life comes back together
Although arranged quite differently.
It is stronger. It is more firm even though held
With moments of sad loneliness
And knowing emptiness.
Yet able to continue. Able to continue living.

Able to know the memories of death,
To know the memories of broken hope.
To be able to say:
"I have felt such bitter pain
I have cried tears that would not stop.
I have wanted to stop living
Only to stop the hurting."

Somehow the miracle of life
Still exists within death.
And I still continue to live
Perhaps to believe in love . . .
As I am able to say:
"My baby has died."

—Gael G. Jarrett

As expressed by Neumann, the "archetype of the way" expresses the "tendency toward consciousness working as an inner law of order in which there is consolidated a superior wisdom that proves to be stronger than the anxiety emerging" (1976, 9). Therefore, despite the conscious desire to escape the pain of grief, the bereaved turn inward toward their sorrow and explore the deep interiority of their loss, where self and soul are battered. Following this first, painful, step of the process, the personal meaning of the loss eventually is realized. The duration of this introverted period varies. For the most part, however, it continues beyond the diminution of the more observable demonstrations of grief. Not as obvious to the outside observer, it is described by the bereaved as a condition of reflection, quietude, fantasizing, or musing, which becomes integrated into the life experience to a deeper degree than was the case before the child's death.

In the second phase of this psychological process, the inner image of the child is born. With the development of the inner image of the actual child, the parent can then remain in relationship to the child until psychologically more able to separate from the literal child. As this inner image becomes more defined, the external searching for the return of the child diminishes and the parent begins to trust again in the incorruptibility of attachment. In the situation of infant loss, the child's image serves as both a means to give the child an identity, to incarnate it, and to enable the parents to manifest their parenthood.

The tension inherent between the conscious longing for the lost child and the reality of the finality of death ultimately activates the transcendent function, which is aimed at restoring balance within the energetic, psychic field.

Just as humans experienced in symbolic ritual the merger or associative connection between the "place" of ritual and the archetype behind it, as in a sacred place upon which a temple is built, so the "image" of the deceased child also finds correspondence with the relevant archetypal imago. The image of the actual child later becomes associated with the archetype of the divine child. This new configuration may ultimately lead to restoring to the bereaved parent those attributes associated with the child. More simply stated, the image of the divine child leads us to what is missing in ourselves. The image is most often incarnated within the dreams of the survivor, and, as Edinger describes it, "each dream can be considered a letter sent to Egypt to awaken us" (1972, 125).

In grief, all that is childlike is gone. Feelings of trust, hope, promise of a future, belief in the mercifulness of God are gravely challenged—if not hopelessly lost. As Hillman states, "Having lost the child, the [mother] has lost the imagination which would be the very way back to it [the childlike]" (1983, 174). The activation of the divine-child archetype reanimates these childlike qualities within the psyche of the parent. The most healing of these qualities include futurity, redemption, growth, joy, vitality for life, curiosity, trust, and openness of feeling. If the conscious attitude of the mourner remains dominated by the need to contain, discipline, limit, judge, or reform the feelings evoked by the inner child, the personal creativity of the mourner is sacrificed in the name of adult propriety.

Such a situation existed for Alice, an analysand of a colleague of mine who was referred to me in order to help her resolve her feelings resulting from a miscarriage several years before. While providing marriage counseling to Alice and her husband, my colleague had observed that Alice was unable to express to her husband her sadness at the early loss of their first and only child. Instead, she was understandably angry toward him, having learned of an extramarital affair he was having just before the miscarriage. The confusion of feelings that Alice suffered, her sadness at losing the child, combined with her feelings of betrayal led her to resolve not to speak to her husband about her grief for the lost child. As she explained to me in our session, "He didn't deserve our daughter. He betrayed us."

Since her husband took her silence as an indication that she had resolved her feelings regarding the miscarriage, he never raised the subject with her. In the ensuing years, Alice guarded her sorrow, and it soon developed into an amalgamated symbol of her husband's insensitivity, her own loss of trust and innocence, and the lack of creativity within their marriage. Inevitably, they grew further apart from one another. Her husband was emotionally isolated from Alice by his guilt, she by her unspoken grief. In the following years their relationship functioned on a mostly practical level, working together in a shared business enterprise but without much intimacy or joy. It was this situation that had brought them into marriage counseling. For the counseling to work however, Alice and her husband needed to escape the bonds of silence and share their vulnerabilities with each other.

When the grieving parent experiences the image of the divine child as psychically real, as existing within, and of value to the healing of grief, the compensatory function of the image is achieved. This process occurs intrapsychically through the energetic principle of enantidromia. Jung described the symbolic image as enantiodromian in structure and thus the symbol itself "presents a rhythm of negative and positive, loss and gain, dark and light. Its beginning is almost invariably characterized by one's getting stuck in some impossible situation, and its goal is illumination or higher consciousness by means of which the initial situation is overcome on a higher level" (1969b, par. 82).

Essential to the stage of Rebirth and the resolution of the mourning is the conscious reintegration of those attributes projected onto or associated with the child which were feared lost. Otherwise, these contents continue to be projected elsewhere and remain unconscious. This is especially likely for those parents who attempt to replace the deceased child too quickly through another pregnancy. In this case the new child becomes the carrier for the unlived-out attributes. Von Franz described this phenomenon as the "wandering of projections." She explained: "If one wants to prevent a renewal of projections, the content must be recognized as psychically real, though not as part of the subject but as an autonomous power." Similarly, integration is understood as the psychological process in which the "hitherto unconscious psychic content is brought repeatedly into view of the conscious ego and recognized as belonging to its own personality" (1980, 13).

The archetypal image of the divine child cannot, however, be entirely integrated and its archetypal core is therefore able to reemerge again in times of future conflict. The divine aspect of the image, however, in association with the image of the actual child, captures the conscious attention of the dreamer and thus awakens the dreamer to the experience of the transpersonal, or imago dei aspect of the Self. Furthermore, this unique Self-generated image is not only the divine child whose attributes are themselves transpersonal, nor is it exclusively a representation of the actual child whose characteristics are, by definition, still developmentally immature. Rather, this Self-generated image is an admixture of both and therefore embraces all things that are deemed childlike in kind. An example of this is seen in another dream provided by Ronda. I have included her own description of the dream and her comments to my interpretation of it as it appeared in an article we collaborated on for *The Loving Arms Newsletter* (Fall 1987).

The dream happened nearly a year after the accident. I had it only once, but was so vivid that I can still recall it in perfect detail. In the dream, I find myself in the little country cemetery where Adam is buried, standing a little way off. Two men, unaware of my presence, are exhuming his grave. They draw the little white coffin out of the ground, set it on the grass and move away to dig another grave. I am aware of birds singing, lilacs blooming close by, and a light breeze.

I approach the box hesitantly, and try the lid, my fingers shaking. It opens easily, almost as if by itself. There in front of me is little Adam. He has not decayed, and his skin looks soft and dewy. He looks so still and beautiful that I cannot resist. My love for him and my desire to touch him overcomes my fear of his death, so I reach in, and tenderly lift him out. I hold his face to mine, and kiss his little cheek and the corner of his mouth. His eyelids flutter! He coughs a little! Then he spits up—not normal milky stuff from a nursing baby, but thicker stuff that is blood-red. I see a building close by, so I carry him inside to clean him up. I see a refrigerator, reach in and draw out a bottle of goat's milk (which is more easily digested than cow's milk—I seem to have injected my nu-

tritional concerns into the dream!). I feel sad that I cannot offer him the breast, but he seems hungry so I give him the bottle. He sucks noisily, and in a moment he is smiling up at me, flashing his brown eyes and flirting a little. In spite of my initial fear and awkwardness, I am charmed. I smile down and tease back, touching his cheeks and eyelids with my lips and fingers. His hair is silky, and he smells warm and sweet.

Suddenly, from out of nowhere, the two men are there. They tell me it is time to put Adam back into his coffin and new grave. I protest—can't they see he is alive now! How can they even think of putting him back into the ground? They shake their heads and look knowingly at one another. They explain, impatiently, that people always do this when a grave is exhumed, but that they always go back to being dead. I have to put him back. They take him out of my arms. The bottle hangs from my hand, empty. I follow them back in stunned silence and watch as they return him to the womb of the earth as I stand helplessly by. Goodbye . . . goodbye . . .

Judith told me that this dream was my way of telling myself that Adam really is dead while allowing me some time to mother Adam as I was never able to since he died before he was born. The two men are symbolic aspects of the Self telling myself that yes, Adam really is dead, but that I truly am a mother. Judith thought that I used this dream to help myself to finally and fully face his death and accept it.

In the three years since Adam died, I have accepted his death. As strange as it may sound, God has somehow caused the most horrifying and traumatic event in my life to become a precious and inexplicably beautiful part of my life. I believe that Judith's interpretation of this particular dream is another piece I can add to the mosaic that God has helped me put together in order to make sense out of nonsense and turn profound grief and pain into joy and a deep inner sense of peace.

In the many dreams I received from parents whose child, or children, have died, the transcendent image was separated from the other representations of the actual child by such circumstances as being bathed in a yellow or bright light and able to stand, walk, or talk despite being an infant. In other dreams the infants or children lovingly inform the parent that they are safe "in heaven," or the children show a sweet and peaceful countenance. The following is an example of this type:

The small cedar chest jewelry box we used to bury our baby in was sitting on a table but the lid was open. I knew we had glued it shut and I was shaken to see it open. When I dared look inside, there was a beautiful, full and round baby, peacefully sleeping and breathing.

The cedar tree is associated with Mary, the Mother of God, because of its enduring beauty, dignity, and strength. Further, cedar pitch was used by the ancients to preserve dead bodies, and it is the cedar that symbolized the fructifying and everlasting nature of the Word, planted by the Lord "as cedar trees beside the water" (de Vries 1974, 89). Thus, the image of the infant in this mother's dream is embraced by the enduring and regenerative symbol of the cedar. Within such a vessel, the coffin itself is transformed from a mere container of the dead to the "vessel of immortality itself." As von Franz explained it, the coffin of the Egyptian and the Canopic jars "which contained the entrails of the deceased are symbols of life's continuation . . . the womb in which the mysterious process of Osiris' rebirth takes place" (1986, 18–19).

This dream, produced by the Self, served several psychological ends simultaneously. First, as a numinous dream it captured the attention of the grieving mother, Wendy, whose loss was then lessened by the realization of her eternal attachment to her lost daughter. Within the matrix of this attachment the mother could then manifest her identity as a parent through the expression of her fondness and love for the child. Furthermore, by "imagining" the child as healthy, "full and round," the compensatory function of the dream is realized, providing the parent with an alternative self-image that could expiate the residue of her guilt. In other words, she can realize that *her* body did not kill or prematurely reject the child. Rather, death did, and death is a primordial force beyond the personal responsibility of the parent. If, on the other hand, the child's death had been due to overt abuse or neglect in pregnancy, as was, for example, the case with another analysand, Sylvia, in her past use of drugs, the parent would first need to accept that measure of personal responsibility for the outcome before being exempt from culpability. However, even under these circumstances, any culpability must be assessed with compassion and awareness of our human fallibility. Although Sylvia's past drug use later contributed to the death of her first child (since by sharing a needle she developed Rh antibodies that later attacked the developing fetus), she was first a victim herself. Her cocaine addiction led her to consequences that she could not have foreseen. In all cases, the preventability of the death is a central feature to the mourning.

Independent of logic, most mourners, and especially parents, are burdened by the incessant fear that in some inexplicable way they had caused the death or failed to prevent it. Such a condition is, in part, created by the natural tandem structure of the archetype itself. Thus, the parents take their identity in part from the condition of the child.

Therefore, if the child is deformed, retarded, or dead, the corresponding parental identity reflects this condition and the parents view themselves as inadequate or bad. As Hillman explains, the tandem or conjoining of symbolic images is "coterminous. The very term 'mother' takes its significance partly from the tandem with the 'child' . . . we are always conjoined" (1983, 175–76). Therefore, to understand the intensity of the interactive field between parent and child, which is itself archetypally structured, we must "analyze, take apart, the interlacing of their plots" (*ibid.*, 175).

Approached from this perspective, the resolution of mourning occurs with the enantiodromian transformation of the image of external, dead child—and this is the essential point—into an internal, healthy child born of imagination itself. This "imagined" child then embodies the creative, childlike wonder of life, and once reanimated and recognized as psychically real, it brings forth those attributes previously experienced as lost within the psyche of the bereaved parent. The parent is no longer trapped within the separating, oppositionality of identification with the either/or polarity of the archetype. The parent is herself not bad (Terrible Mother) because the child was all good (Divine Child). Nor is the child all bad (Terrible Child) while the parent is all good (Divine Victim). They are both, by nature, good and bad. Within this context the development of the imagined child in this dream is itself both bad by virtue of being dead and good by virtue of being imaged as "full and round, peacefully sleeping and breathing," and the ambivalence of the imago is symbolically resolved. With the restoration of the imagination to the parent, the parent can begin to reexperience the qualities of imagination itself, specifically, a sense of future and hope. Furthermore, once the childlike qualities projected onto the child are recognized as also residing within the parent's psyche, the parent can return more openly toward life, reexperiencing joy, possibility, growth, trust, and love. This regenerative and healing function of the Self, as supported by Knapp's findings, also corresponds to the psychological development of a religious attitude, culminating in a revitalization of religious beliefs, a tolerance toward the suffering of others, and a keen appreciation for the value of life.

In this final stage of Rebirth in the archetypal paradigm of mourning, the grieving parents arrive at a "meaning" for their tragic loss, which may renew and deepen a preexisting religious belief. In other instances it remains less structured. But in all cases, it acknowledges a conscious recognition of the transpersonal force at work in their lives. As Emerson describes it:

The secret of the world is the tie between the person and event. . . . The soul contains the event that shall befall it. . . . The event is the print of your form. Events grow on the same stem with persons. (As quoted in Edinger 1972, 101)

The parents, released from the need to locate the lost personal attributes within the actual child itself, now begin to trust in the incorruptibility of their affection and their connection to the inner, imaged child. This same incorruptibility is expressed in Isaiah 43:2–4, which also profoundly parallels the mourning process itself and the need to trust in its natural unfolding:

When you pass through the waters I will be with you; and through the rivers, they shall not overwhelm you; when you walk through fire you shall not be burned, and the flame shall not consume you. . . . For I am the LORD *your God. . . . Because you are precious in my eyes, and honored, and I love you, I give men in return for you, peoples in exchange for your life.*

The mystery of transformation may be difficult for many parents to convey in words and therefore it may remain experienced as only a feeling or a belief, but this same difficulty is also shared by Jung when he writes to a friend whose child died:

What happens after death is so unspeakably glorious that our imagination and our feelings do not suffice to form even an approximate conception of it. . . . A child enters [a] sublimity and there detaches himself from this world more quickly than the aged. So easily does he become what you also are that he apparently vanishes. The dissolution of our timebound form in eternity brings no less meaning. Rather does the little finger know itself a member of the hand. (As quoted in von Franz 1984, 143)

In conclusion, the parents whose grief is resolved have been, through the suffering of the experience, made more conscious of the intensity of their enduring attachments, of the depth of their dark journey of mourning and the healing that can occur when its natural progression is allowed to unfold. Through their experience, they have encountered deeper aspects of themselves than they might otherwise have known. In addition, as supported by Knapp's findings, they are less afraid of their own death. Though none would hope to suffer the experience again, they have nonetheless gained from it. With the restoration of the inner "imaged" child now understood as an enduring part of themselves, the wound is healed, as seen in the poem by Gael Jarrett quoted in full previously:

> Life comes back together
> Although arranged quite differently.
> It is stronger. It is more firm even though held
> With moments of sad loneliness
> And knowing emptiness.
> Yet able to continue. Able to continue living.
>
> Able to know the memories of death,
> To know the memories of broken hope.
> To be able to say:
> "I have felt such bitter pain
> I have cried tears that would not stop.
> I have wanted to stop living
> Only to stop the hurting."
>
> Somehow the miracle of life
> Still exists within death.
> And I still continue to live
> Perhaps to believe in love . . .
> As I am able to say:
> "My baby has died."

At this concluding phase of the archetypal paradigm of mourning, mythically the goddess herself is reborn. The human Mary, for example, is assumed into Heaven, where, reunited with her son, she resides as the Queen of Heaven, so entitled "for the burden she bore." For her human counterpart, however, the rebirth is experienced as the apprehension of the meaning of the loss which results in an expansion of the conscious personality and a deepening within the ego-Self interactive field.

Chapter 7

Implications for Clinical Practice

I have always enjoyed these summer evenings, daydreaming out the window about a dark-haired little boy screaming his pleasure as he skims down that slide. It's been a year since Adam died. It's strange how different I am now. I understand the temptation to forget but, for me, forgetting Adam would be worse than Adam dying. I speak his name whenever I can, delighting in my motherhood. For although he never spoke a word to me, his life and death have spoken volumes. No, things are not as they were, nor as I had hoped. I would rather have Adam living, yet I thank God for the meaning He has brought out of our love. Death had cheated me of Adam's life, but I will not lie down and die with him. I will cheat death . . . perhaps you too will do the same.

Ronda Chinn
Loving Arms Newsletter
(Nov. 1985)

In the preceding chapters, I have attempted to illustrate the process of the archetypal unfolding of mourning as it is experienced by the survivors of the tragic death of a child. One intent I had for this work was to amplify the inadequacies of a traditional ego psychology in addressing the core issue of personal meaning as raised by the child's death. Another was to inveigh against the secularization of psychology, to bring to a level of awareness the fissure that exists within the "healing" arts—the fissure between secular psychology, on the one hand, and religion, on the other, and the effect of this fissure on the subject of grief. But Jung's psychology reunites these seemingly opposing perspectives into a Self-psychology that bridges the inner–outer, psychology–theology split present in our modern Western culture. From the perspective of a Self-psychology, the incorruptibility of our spiritual and psychological connections to one another is given psychological reality. It was in 1909 that Jung first asserted his position that the archetype "exerts a magical hold" upon the interactive field of the parent–child matrix. Separation and death, more than any other life situation, illustrates the intensity of that "magical" hold and the a priori nature of the attachment bond. When the archetypal intent to manifest itself through the attachment is thwarted, as with a death of a child, the experience is as traumatic as was the original expulsion from the Garden to our ancestors. The secularization of psychology, combined with the patriarchal religious trends of our times, has resulted in the wholesale collective disenfranchisement from "natural life and matter, of mundane experience, and the body. Concrete reality, as we encounter it, is increasingly considered devoid of the spirit and opposed to it" (Whitmont 1984, 125).

The testimonies of these bereaved parents not only dramatize the difficulties of their adaptation to the external loss, but also the veracity and depth of the fundamental human need to comprehend the meaning of the loss. As Eliade explained it, "suffering, whatever its nature and whatever its apparent cause, had a meaning" to early humans and was "perturbing only insofar as its cause remained undiscovered. By connecting suffering to the archetypal realm, man was able to endow his search for meaning with a reality and normality" (1954, 96–99). Modern psychology, however, derived as it is from its Freudian origins, cannot escape its tendency to pathologize grief and render it, at least in part, equivalent to neurotic suffering. Furthermore, within the Freudian framework of mental economics, we are led to the fallacy of the interchangeability of the objects toward which our libido or psychic energy is directed. As Marris clarifies it:

> As soon as we treat unique relationships as the idiosyncratic expression of generalizable needs, we risk imposing a logic whereby it ought to be possible to supply an alternative satisfaction of that need. Since mourners repudiate any such substitution, their behavior looks puzzling, irrational, and by a short step, morbid. (As quoted in Parkes 1972, 186).

The tragic experience of these parents teaches us that love itself is enduring and that each love expressed toward varying objects has its own form, which seeks to be realized. *Until that realization is made conscious and given meaning, the transformation of mourning cannot be fully accomplished.*

To this end, analytical psychology is better suited. Given its inclusion of unconscious material into the therapeutic framework and its treating of the whole psyche in accordance with the principle of individuation, analytical psychology extends beyond the adjustment objective of ego psychology and avails the bereaved of the regenerative capacity of the Self.

Therapists routinely confront the agony of grief springing from many sources. However, when grief is born from the premature death of a child, it is most intense. Well-intentioned sympathy aimed at comforting the bereaved, although helpful, is certainly not enough to quiet the tide of remorse. The bereaved parent struggles daily to embrace the memories of the deceased child, much as Isis re-membered the broken body of her son Osiris. Through this mythical act, both the goddess and her son were reborn and a new dimension within the myth and the consciousness of man was created. Similarly, this same archetypal paradigm compels the parents to vow never to forget, to relive the horror of the death repeatedly, and eventually to discover its meaning to their personal life.

One cannot discuss a dead child, whether miscarried, aborted, stillborn, diseased, or killed, without also activating the archetypal associations with it, which are, by nature, powerful. As had already been explained, the image of the dead child constellates feelings of inadequacy, shame, bodily defect, corruptibility of flesh, lost hope, lost future, and emptiness. The constellation of these feelings, however, is not confined only to the parents. As with any archetypal content, the feelings are also activated within those around the parents. Because of the inherent repulsion of facing such images, both the parents and their associates cannot help but want to turn away from the image of the dead child. For the parent, the turning away involves an intense struggle between recalling the event and the child, on the one hand, and desiring to forget it, on the other. This struggle cannot be avoided. However, even within the tolerant acceptance of the consulting room, where so many torments are openly revealed and discussed, the death of a child presents an arduous challenge of forebearance for both the analyst and the patient.

I have often been impressed by how frequently the reproductive histories of parents have remained unacknowledged, the unfortunate sentiment being that childbearing histories are most often of interest only to gynecologists and obstetricians. Despite an otherwise thorough case anamnesis, therapists may omit noting reproductive losses, disregarding their etiological influence and viewing them merely as an unfortunate but short-term loss from which the patient readily recovers. This patent collective disregard for the loss of a child in early pregnancy is an insidious denial. After suffering a miscarriage, stillbirth, or neonatal loss, parents are typically reminded that it was better to have lost the child early in term since it was, to begin with, defective. The evidence provided by these parents, however, repudiates the irrelevance attributed to such losses. Regardless of the shortness of the life, the parental attachment had already begun. According to MacFarlane, 49 percent of women located the beginning of their affection for their future child before its birth (as quoted in Kitzinger 1978). Regardless of the possibility of their having other children, parents are understandably disturbed whenever it is suggested that should they turn away from their grief or their need to complete the parental task of bringing the dead child into psychological reality. Jung regarded taking a thorough anamnesis of the patient's history as essential:

> *In many cases . . . the patient who comes to us has a story that is* not told, *and which as a rule no one knows of. To my mind therapy only begins after the investigation of that wholly personal story. It is the patient's secret, the rock against which he is shattered. If I know his secret story, I have the key to the treatment.* (Emphasis added, 1961, 117)

As Stein elaborates, "Assembling and re-experiencing the 'story that is not told'—both its conscious and unconscious components—belongs to what Jung called . . . confession and elucidation. . . . The phase of confession . . . reveals the part of the story that the patient *can tell but often hasn't because of a sense of shame or guilt*" (emphasis added, 1985, 33).

When dealing with a child's death, the therapeutic task at hand is not only to be supportive or to prematurely direct the focus toward the issue of meaning. The initial therapeutic task must be aimed toward the conscious acceptance of the loss. To this end, the reality of the child's life, however short, must be acknowledged by actively developing an identity for the child through giving him or her a name and character in accordance with the parents' hopes and expectations for the young life. It is not uncommon for parents to refer to such losses as "my first miscarriage" or "the loss," but a gentle reference to the child by name serves to keep the parent in relationship with the child and augments both the attachment and the eventual letting go.

In cases where the loss is less immediate, occurring some time in the past, it is important to not assume that its not having been reported by the analysand meant that the experience held little significance. Rather, the pervasive shame inherent with infant and child death, combined with the adaptive urges of the ego, is such that a past death or miscarriage may never be raised voluntarily. Even within the process of amplifying a dream image of an infant or child, I have been impressed that the association of that image to an actual miscarried or stillborn child in a patient's history may not be made by the dreamer. If this association is not made, such a dream image can only be understood as a subjective component of the dreamer's own personality; therefore, the unconscious intent to resolve the remnants of mourning remains unrecognized. For example, in a speech of a colleague, I heard the analyst describe an analysand who was "repeatedly complaining regarding the death of a stillborn child which occurred over two years ago." The analyst responded to this "complaining" by interpreting it as an unconscious desire of the client to elicit from the analyst a sympathetic stance. Thus, treated too literally within the transference/countertransference interaction, the psychological intent of the mother's "complaining" was diluted. From my perspective, this analysand may have in fact been soliciting a sympathetic "mother" response from the analyst which would then open a "maternal" space for discussion within the analytical relationship for the still-lingering effect of mourning upon the woman. Without acknowledging the reality of the child, its image is analogous to a negative spirit who, unable to enter the afterlife, then haunts the mother.

The process of psychologically embodying or incarnating the child image must include a willingness on the part of the therapist to face the disturbing facts of its death. If the death occurs in pregnancy or shortly thereafter, the patients should be supported in their desire to have evidence of the child, such as having a photo taken, naming the child, burying it ceremoniously, and talking about it. (With older children, where an extant history of such remembrances already exists, some aspects of this need not be replicated.) However, the circumstances of the baby's death, including, for example, the autopsy results, should be matter of factly discussed. Becoming informed of the medical reasons causing the death, the parents enact the concern and interest inherent in the parental role. This may be the only direct knowledge of their child that they have and because of this it is common that many become experts on their particular kind of loss, whether it be encephaly, ectopic, hypoxia, or Rh disease. Not only does this knowledge help keep them in relationship to their child, but it also helps mitigate their helplessness and diminish their feelings of recrimination.

Experiencing directly the source of another's sorrow can be difficult.

As with all material of its kind, the constellation of powerful death imagery also affects the therapist, who then is subject to the constellation of associated death-experiences within herself. It is therefore necessary for the analyst to be conscious of the nature of personal losses and to differentiate the patient's losses from those suffered by the analyst so that stereotypic generalizations are not needlessly projected onto the mourner. As Knapp's findings suggest, the circumstances of the child's death result in a unique patterning of the mourning itself. Each mourning process has its own natural course of unfolding and should not be overly constrained by external expectations regarding appropriate length or extent of the suffering. However, I have attempted to illustrate that the common experience of mourning extends beyond a superficial similarity in human behavior. Such commonality of experience suggests, in my opinion, the influence of the archetypal structure underlying it. Archetypes, or a priori modes of human perception, have no solid content and are not fixed symbols. According to Jung, "They acquire solidity, influence, and eventual consciousness in the encounter with empirical facts, which touch the unconscious aptitude and quicken it to life" (1953, par. 300). The archetypal endowment, as Stevens (1982, 39) explains it, is common to all humankind, yet each person experiences it in his or her own particular way.

Once the actual death of the child has been given reality and acceptance, the parents are then allowed to express their grief honestly and without undue restraint. Because of the detailed description of the normal emotional process of mourning already established through the work of thanatological researchers, the course of its expression is relatively predictable. Thus, we can anticipate without alarm the presence of labile moods, tearfulness, anger, apathy toward the matters of life, sleeplessness, and so forth. However, the genuine risks activated by the urge of suicide or self-injury must be assessed and, if necessary, preventive action taken. In this early phase of the treatment, the stabilizing support by the therapist predominates. At this juncture, it is premature to introduce much in the way of understanding the personal meaning of the loss, even if the topic is raised by the analysand. More important is conveying the genuine conviction that the meaning will ultimately make itself known and that the distressing symptoms will abate. As Knapp suggests, "Although we may feel obliged to attempt to answer the unyielding question of 'Why, why did this happen?' more likely this question is, at this stage, merely seeking our approval that it is a legitimate question to ask" (1986, 189).

Because of the intensity of mourning, it is judicious to recognize the limits of support a therapist can realistically provide. Therefore it is helpful to augment the therapy with a support group for parents who have lost children. The contribution of such groups to healing is considerable. Through the participatory format of these groups, the sharing of similar experiences helps normalize the experience and reduce isolation.

Of particular relevance to the transference/countertransference relationship is the constellation of the archetypal images of death and mourning as these images affect the parent-child paradigm within the analytical setting. For the analysand, issues of failure and inadequacy will undoubtedly arise, but these feelings will need to be differentiated from the archetypal motifs related to them. Such an amplifying process, however, may have an intensifying effect upon the emotions themselves, which the analysand may temporarily regret, and given the power of these images, the sorrow that was diminished may again reopen with renewed intensity. This may be unconsciously experienced by the analysand as an act of cruelty on the therapist's part and therefore should be directed in accordance with the emergence of the patient's own psychological material. *But it is not to be avoided.* By attending to both the external adjustment of the analysand and the content of their dreams, the clinician can assess the appropriateness of raising such difficult material. Given the compensatory and self-regulating aspect of dreams, the mandate to make conscious certain aspects of the loss is generated from the self; therefore the therapist need not be overly zealous in imposing his or her expectations regarding time or "progress" in the resolution of grief. Although the projection of cruelty upon the analyst presents an issue that must be addressed, such a projection also initiates the analysand's freedom from the internal dominance of the lost child, which of course, serves a therapeutic function in eventual rapprochement.

The constellation of the image of the dead child can exert a powerful effect upon the analytical relationship. It may, for example, contaminate a previously trusting and viable relationship with feelings of hopelessness, stagnation, impermanence, and corruptibility. The therapy may now be experienced as insufficient to the task, unable to proceed beyond the subject of death and grief. At these times, the analysand may attempt to compensate for the heavy emotional tone by apologizing for his or her tears or anger, just as a parent apologizes for a child's unruly behavior in public. Such an affectual climate may also cause the patient to feel that the analyst does not want to endure these emotions and might secretly be wanting (or intending?) to terminate. Although the therapist may have no intention of terminating, the intensity of the experience should be acknowledged so as to not alienate the patient needlessly through a persona of impenetrable strength and fortitude. Such a persona only causes the analysand to feel weak in contrast, and fosters either dependency or an unconscious desire to sabotage the analyst by exposing the professional's weaknesses.

The urge for the parent to move away from the morbid imagery of the child's death is strong. Such attempts at denial can be seen either in disregarding its effects altogether or in idealizing the child and thereby denying the negativity of its death. Such a denial is also possible for the analyst, and when it exists, the analyst unconsciously collaborates with the patient's denial system and impedes recovery.

Similarly, too swiftly turning toward the search for meaning or the transcendent image of the child is also a defense strategy. Meaning, as understood within Jung's Self-psychology, is revealed in accordance to its own timing. The alchemist, who, by analogy, is like the analyst, cannot transform the base material, the *prima materia*, into the Philosopher's Stone without first proceeding through a purposeful series of operations upon it—what Edinger terms *calcinatio, solutio, coagulatio, sublimatio, mortefactio, separatio,* and *coniunctio.*

The analytical relationship can aid parents in the task of establishing their own identities as parents, regardless of the presence of other surviving children. It is therefore of critical importance that the analyst reflect the patient's symbolic parenthood, viewing it as psychically real and thereby enabling the patient to claim it as his or her own. If the parenthood remains unacknowledged, it becomes an orphan, seeking the reflection of itself in the face of everyone encountered.

An example of such mislocation of parental attachment occurred with Martha. I first met her in 1979 when she came to me suffering from depression. After a year and a half of therapy, Martha had made significant progress in establishing a more independent life for herself, which included moving away from living with her mother on whom she had grown overly dependent. She terminated her therapy shortly before I left for Zurich to take up my analytic training. Upon my return to this country three years later, Martha again contacted me. In the time I had been away, Martha had decided to have a child and had become pregnant but had lost the baby at birth. Now, one year later, Martha had taken up with a younger, homosexual man. However, even though the relationship had become difficult she felt compelled to remain in it. It seemed to have a magical hold upon her. Despite her own better judgment, or her anger that he cared little for her needs, she persisted. Due to the young man's homosexuality, their relationship was primarily organized around Martha's need to be maternal and the young man's childish behavior. Martha indulged him in every way, such as talking with him about his problems at all hours of the night. Needless to say, the relationship was exhausting her. However, she was caught in an unconscious and compulsive need to see herself as a mother. To this end, she had unconsciously chosen an immature man to mother. Quite literally, he was like an infant who needed night feedings and her constant attention. In time, Martha was able to break her attachment to him but only after becoming conscious of how her need to mother had been misdirected toward her friend. Within the analysis, Martha returned her attention to the lost baby and her unresolved grief.

By becoming conscious of her unrequited love and the true object her love sought, it was less likely to be unconsciously misplaced onto others. It is through the maintenance of the inner image of the child that the parent can symbolically manifest parenthood. As Lewis described it, in the case of a mother who was denied the opportunity to see or hold her dead child, her dreams then enacted this event for her:

> *This is a nice example of the healing of dreams. In her dream the mother was able to hold the baby she had not held. In her imagination she "brought her baby back to death"; in her dreams her stillborn baby became real in her arms. . . . It is natural for a bereaved mother to hold her baby herself.* (As quoted in Klaus and Kennell 1983, 168)

It is a belief well documented in history and mythology that facing the corpse of a dead child is too difficult for a parent to experience. Such an encounter, however, is within the realm of love, and as an act, it expresses the natural need to embrace what is lost. Mythically, it is the lesson of the Fisher King in the myth of Isis and Osiris. The Fisher King was the child who was taken by Isis, who later witnessed her grief when she released her son's body from its coffin. The Fisher is also called Maneros, according to Plutarch, which means "the understanding of Love" (Harding 1971, 174). Similarly, in the *Legends of the Madonna* (1904), it is written:

When Joseph of Arimathea and Nicodemus wrenched out the nails which fastened the hands of the Lord to the cross, St. John *took them away secretly that his mother might not see them.* And then while Nicodemus drew forth the nails which fastened his feet, Joseph sustained the body, so that the arms hung over his shoulder. And *the afflicted mother, seeing this arose and she took the bleeding hands of her Son and she clasped them in her own, and kissed them tenderly.* (Jameson 1904, 408)

Nearly all of the parents with whom I spoke reported that the opportunity to hold their dead child was helpful to the resolution of their mourning. Those who were denied this generally regretted it. Patty, for example, whom I described earlier in the text, felt shamed by her husband from examining the body of her daughter, the surviving twin who died 44 hours after delivery. When the clothed infant's body was presented to her, Patty began to undress her but stopped when she observed the appalled shock of her husband's expression. Patty explained that seeing her daughter, but having been unable to touch her because of the incubator and life-support systems, caused her to want to examine her more closely, and feel the softness of her skin upon her own. "I know he thought this was perverted or morbid," she added, "but I just wanted to know what she looked like."

The analytical relationship, offered as a vessel or sacred place for the grief can be of vital help in making conscious the regenerative and healing capacity of the Self. Within this sacred place, the bereaved parent awaits the dream which then helps in acknowledging the reality of the loss while still maintaining a psychological connection to the child. This tension of the desire to regain the child and the reality of the loss activate the transcendent function.

The transcendent image of the child, represented as a unifying amalgam of both the "divine" aspect of the child archetype and the actual child, then initiates the enantiodromian progression of psychic energy. Thus, the search for the external object is transformed into an inner search that produces a reflective attitude. Once these lost attributes are consciously known as also residing within the subject's own psyche, the child image then functions as a psychopomp, unifying the conscious and unconscious realms. This process results in a restoration within the ego-Self axis while simultaneously expanding the breadth of consciousness. Ultimately, as the meanings attached to the child are made conscious, those attributes which were feared permanently lost are regained and the parent can return to life with hope, imagination, trust, and an openness toward experience.

It is this natural psychological process, directed by the Self, which can culminate in the regeneration of a religious attitude, or belief, the expansion of tolerance, and the revaluing of life and intimacy, as reported by the majority of the parents in Knapp's study and as expressed by the parents with whom I have had contact.

Mary, a mother who became a support parent to others who have suffered losses, described the transformation of her challenged faith in her contribution to the *Loving Arms Newsletter* (May 1986). She wrote that following the stillbirth of her second son Joshua, she felt that

> *I couldn't question my faith in God and His plan for my life. After a few months, it became apparent to me that I couldn't go on living like that. I was angry with God and I was even more angry with myself for being angry with God. It was disconcerting to find that I couldn't go to church any more without crying. Later, I had to let go of the bitterness. During this time, I questioned many of my previous beliefs about God which in turn changed my life in many positive ways. Today I find that my faith has not only increased, but also my understanding of His love is clear because I questioned Him.*

Mary's experience evokes a parallel with Job's challenge to God's divine benevolence, a subject of great interest to Jung. In his *Answer to Job* (1969, par. 757) Jung argued that genuine faith could only be experienced through an encounter with the dark side of God which challenges believers' naive trust in God's omnipotent benevolence. He writes:

> *Faith is certainly right when it impresses on humankind's mind and heart how infinitely far away and inaccessible God is; but it also teaches his nearness, his immediate presence,* and it is just this nearness which has to be empirically real *if it is not to lose all significance.* Only that which acts upon me do I recognize as real and actual. *But that which has no effect upon me might as well not exist.* (Emphasis added, *ibid.*)

Similarly Ronda, the woman described earlier whose son Adam was killed in a car accident while she was in the final month of pregnancy, describes the challenge to her faith and the strength that the tragedy added to her life. She wrote:

> *It's strange how different I am now. To go on for me means that although Adam's death will last for the rest of my life, I must not allow it to take from me any more than Adam itself. I cannot allow death to become a festering wound that would eventually sap the life away from me in a kind of living death. There are battles to be fought every day. I understand the temptation to forget, but for me, forgetting Adam would seem worse than Adam dying. I am proud of him . . . and, I speak his name whenever I can, delighting in my motherhood, proud as any mother of a living child. Maybe prouder. For although he never spoke a word to*

me, his life and death have spoken volumes. God has used the grief and
sorrow to create a new awareness in me of the value of a person, a
moment. It is harder to take my loved ones for granted; easier to choose
the important thing instead of the urgent one.

As the testimony of bereaved parents attests, having sustained the ordeal they were strengthened. Having found personal meaning from the loss, their suffering was no longer meaningless but instead brought them closer to the imago-dei aspect of the Self, also known as God.

Glossary of Jungian Terms

Adaptation   A component of individuation, distinguished from conformism and indicating a balancing of internal and external factors (Samuels et al. 1986, 10). Either a failure to adapt or a one-sided adaptation to external or inner objectives was viewed by Jung as one cause of neurosis.

Alchemy   The practice from the fifteenth and sixteenth centuries that sought to transform a base material (*prima materia*) into something more valuable, symbolically changing matter into spirit (Samuels et al. 1986, 12). This transformative process, which developed through a purposeful series of operations, was used by Jung as a metaphor for analysis and the development of consciousness. Each alchemical operation, as well as the relationship between the alchemist and the material, parallels the tasks of differentiating the contents of the psyche in accordance with the principle of INDIVIDUATION.

Analytical psychology   The term coined by Jung in 1913 for his theory, which distinguished his psychology from Freud's psychoanalytic movement.

Anamnesis   Along with confession and elucidation, this is a part of the analytic process and involves a recollection, or a recalling to memory.

Archetype   An original model or type on which similar things are patterned. This is an inherent part of the psyche that organizes human experience into typical patterns that cluster around such universal experiences as birth, death, and marriage, and other rites of passage. According to Samuels et al., archetypes "wait to be realized in the personality, are capable of infinite variation, and carry a strong energy which arouses affect" (1986, 26–27). An archetype forms the center of each complex. An unconscious identification with an archetype can dominate the personality to such an extent that free will is limited and individual identity is, in varying degrees, lost. In contrast, a conscious relationship with the archetypal image inhibits such INFLATION and deepens the personality while at the same time restoring flexibility to it.

Cognitive dissonance   A form of psychological conflict between a subjective inner image or idea and its objective reality, as when an imaged child is discordant with the actual child.

Collective unconscious   Jung's term for the part of the unconscious that consists of the universal experiences of humankind (see ARCHE-TYPES) and is distinct from the personal unconscious which, in contrast, is composed of personal memories and experiences.

Complex   According to Jung, the complex is a fragmentary personality, organized around an archetypal core, associated with memories, ideas, feelings, and experiences which share a common feeling tone. Complexes have the ability to disturb consciousness, inhibit or distort memory, and influence behavior. The content of the GREAT MOTHER ARCHETYPE, for example, combined with one's experience of a personal mother characterizes the nature of an individual mother's complex.

Coniunctio   Represented as the sacred marriage between the masculine and the feminine, it is the alchemical symbol for the union of opposites. The product of this sacred union, the Divine Child, symbolizes the rejuvenating potential for greater wholeness.

Countertransference   An unconscious projection by an analyst onto the analysand.

Decathexis   A Freudian term describing the withdrawal of libido or psychic energy away from a person, object, or idea.

Divine-Child archetype   Representing wholeness, futurity, imagination, the fructifying new life within the psyche, this ARCHETYPE also serves as a mediating principle between the conscious and unconscious realms.

Doctrines

> **Immaculate Conception:** The Roman Catholic doctrine that the Virgin Mary was conceived in her mother's womb free from original sin.

> **Assumption of the Virgin** (*Assumptio Mariae*): Roman Catholic doctrine referring to the bodily taking up of the Virgin Mary into Heaven after her death. A psychological symbol for the transformation of sorrow within the human personality.

Earth Mother   The elemental symbol of Mother Nature, which, when constellated in pregnancy, represents the containing, nurturing aspect (see GREAT MOTHER ARCHETYPE); at her negative pole, she represents death (see TERRIBLE MOTHER ARCHETYPE).

Ego   The center of consciousness, which, as defined by Jung, is only a part of the whole psyche and not in control of it.

Ego psychology A generic term for those psychologies that regard the EGO as the supreme regulating agent of the psyche. Such psychologies, originating from a Freudian legacy, view the unconscious as a repository of primitive, instinctual drives and personal memories and do not attribute to it any regenerative capacity.

Ego-Self axis A term coined by Edinger (1972) referring to the relationship between the EGO as the center of consciousness and the Self as the center of the whole psyche. Jung viewed the ego and the unconscious as interdependent. According to Samuels et al., the unconscious needs the ego's "analysing powers and its capacity to facilitate independent living" while the Self offers the ego "life lived at greater depth and at a greater level of integration" (1986, 52).

Enantiodromia A "running contrariwise," indicating that everything tends, sooner or later, to go over to its opposite (Samuels et al. 1986, 53).

Great Mother archetype The name given to "the general images drawn from the collective, cultural experience" of the maternal principle (Samuels et al. 1986, 62). Structured dualistically, as are all archetypes, the Great Mother archetype possesses both negative and positive attributes, which are each represented in mythic-religious themes and iconography. According to Jung, the personal mother is perceived by the child in association with its archetypal counterpart, causing the magical hold between the mother and child to be intensified. It is through this archetypal projection that the child first experiences the Self, which is initially projected upon the mother. (See TERRIBLE MOTHER ARCHETYPE.)

Hieros gamos (sacred union) The wedding of the gods, which is symbolized in alchemy as the *coniunctio*.

Imago This is a term used by Jung to refer to the inner image of a person or experience which is not equivalent to the actual person or event and is intensified by the archetype associated with it.

Imago-Dei From the Latin, meaning "the image of God."

Individuation A movement toward wholeness which is directed by the Self. A major contribution by Jung to the theories of personality development, in which he posits an inherent, underlying drive toward wholeness within the psyche which proceeds independent of conscious will. A conscious collaboration with this natural unfolding, however, is the aim of analysis.

Inflation The term applied to the psychological condition in which the ego has become identified with archetypal contents. Under such conditions, free will is diminished, and the person acts as if he or she actually possessed archetypal attributes such as those seen in self-aggrandizing or self-defeating persons. Inflation may be merely transitory or it may be fixated identification. In all instances, it is delusional and causes a false sense of inherent goodness or badness.

Labile A psychological term referring to unpredictable and random changes in mood.

Libido A term used by Freud to define the energy principle, which he regarded as sexual in nature. Although Jung also used this term, he eventually came to prefer "psychic energy," which he thought was less specifically sexual and thereby more accurately descriptive of a general energetic force.

Liminality A term describing a transitional place or condition, a threshold experience. It represents an in-between period, as with adolescence being in between childhood and adulthood.

Liquefactio An alchemical process in which water is applied to the material in order to begin a process of dissolution. This corresponds psychologically to the changes in the evolution of mourning as the mourning is accompanied by tears.

Persona This is Jung's term for a person's social identity, for the "face we show the world." It is derived from the Latin for "mask" and is a necessary development of the personality (see ADAPTATION). Too close an identification with the persona, however, results in a lack of depth and rigidity, which can be seen in persons who depend upon their occupations, roles, and titles for their identity and sense of self-worth.

Participation mystique This refers to an unconscious identification between subject and object, where sufficient differentiation between self and other is lacking. It is inherent in all forms of projection in which attributes belonging to the self are projected onto another. It is also a condition that Jung used to describe the quality of attachment of the infant to its mother.

Psychopomp As described by Samuels et al., it is "the figure which guides the soul at times of initiation and transition" (1986, 122).

Self The central, organizing archetype of the psyche. The transpersonal element that seeks uniformity, balance, and wholeness between the conscious and unconscious realms, it is also the architect of dreams, COMPLEXES, and ARCHETYPES.

Shadow What Jung termed "the thing a person has no wish to be" (CW 15, par. 470) is the dark side representing the rejected instincts and other elements of one's personality. The shadow represents human evil but also contains elements of the personality that are not inherently bad but have been rejected so as to adapt to a particular environment.

Shadow Grief A term developed by Pepper and Knapp (1980) describing the lingering and chronic grief that persists in parent survivors who suffer childbearing losses. It is characterized by emotional dullness, an ache in the background of one's feelings (Knapp 1986, 41), and a sensitivity to stimuli associated with the child, which reawaken the feelings of loss and grief.

Shamanism A form of spiritualism, such as that practiced among certain North American Indian tribes, as in the form of a medicine man. The shaman is thought to possess the power to ascend and descend between earth and the spirit world.

Synchronicity This is a term coined by Jung to refer to an acausal connecting principle. Typically it refers to a meaningful relation between an "inner event," such as a dream, and an "outer event." This is a meaningful coincidence. Jung understood miracles and parapsychological phenomena to be synchronistic events.

Terrible Mother archetype The negative pole of the GREAT MOTHER ARCHETYPE represented by figures that symbolize the death-dealing aspects of Mother Nature. These are impersonal, unrelated aspects of the feminine. In fairy tales and in folklore this is represented by the witch or the evil stepmother.

Transference This is an unconscious projection by an analysand into the analyst, usually of a parental nature, but not invariably. Any COMPLEX or ARCHETYPE may be projected in the transference.

Transcendent function This term refers to the capacity of the Self to produce uniting symbols that bridge the conscious and unconscious realms and resolve tensions within the psychic system.

Glossary of Childbearing (Loss) Terms

D & C   A surgical procedure (dilation and curettage) performed after a miscarriage to cleanse and cauterize the uterus.

Ectopic pregnancy   A pregnancy that occurs when the fertilized egg settles outside the uterus, often in a Fallopian tube.

Hypoxia   This is a condition in which there is insufficient oxygen in the body.

Miscarriage   The condition occurring with the premature expulsion of a nonviable fetus from the uterus, after three months and before seven months. It is also refered to as "a spotaneous abortion."

Neonatal   Having to do with the newborn, or neonate.

Neonatal death   A loss occurring between birth and four weeks after birth.

Perinatal death   A loss occurring at about the time of birth.

Postpartum depression   A despondency occurring during the first six weeks after childbirth.

Rh disease   A disease in which the mother's sensitized immune system attacks the red blood cells of the fetus.

SIDS   An acronym for Sudden Infant Death Syndrome.

Still birth   A birth in which the baby is born dead.

Bibliography

Aries, P. *The Hour of Our Death*. New York: Alfred A. Knopf, 1981.

Balint, M. *The Basic Fault*. New York: Brunner/Mazel, 1968.

Becker, E. *The Denial of Death*. New York: MacMillan, 1973.

Berezin, N. *After a Loss in Pregnancy*. New York: Simon and Schuster, 1982.

Berry-Hillman, P. *Echo's Subtle Body*. Zurich: Spring Publications, 1982.

———. Some Dream Motifs Accompanying the "Abandonment" of an Analytic Practice. *Chiron: A Review of Jungian Analysis* 1985:87–99.

Boer, C., trans. *Hymn to Demeter—The Homeric Hymns*, 2nd ed. Zurich: Spring Publications, 1979.

Boulding, K. *The Image*. Ann Arbor: University of Michigan Press, 1956.

Bowlby, J. *Attachment*. London: Hogarth Press and The Institute of Psychoanalysis, 1969.

———. *Separation: Anxiety and Anger*. New York: Basic Books, Inc., 1973.

———. *Loss, Sadness and Depression*. New York: Basic Books, Inc., 1980.

Bozarth-Campbell, A. *Life Is Goodbye, Life Is Hello*. Minneapolis: CompCare Publications, 1982.

Brown, C., ed. *Religious Lyrics of the Fifteenth Century*. Oxford: Oxford University Press, 1930.

Budge, E. A. W. *Osiris and the Egyptian Resurrection*, vol. 1. New York: Dover Publications, 1973.

Cameron, N. *Personality Development and Psychopathology*. Boston: Houghton Mifflin & Co., 1963.

Conze, E. *Buddhist Scriptures*. Penguin Books, 1956.

Corbett, L. *Suffering and Incarnation: A Study in the Religious Function of the Psyche*. Unpublished thesis, C. G. Jung Institute of Chicago, 1986.

Corbin, H. *Mundas Imaginalis or the Imaginary and the Imagined*. Zurich: Spring Publications, 1972.

Cornes, T. O. Symbol and Ritual in Melancholia: The Archetype of the Divine Victim. *Chiron: A Review of Jungian Analysis* 1985:203–22.

Davidson, A. D. Disaster: Coping with Stress. *Police Stress* 1 (1979):20–22.

Edinger, E. F. *Ego and Archetype*. New York: Penguin Books, 1972.

———. *Anatomy of the Psyche: Alchemical Symbolism in Psychotherapy*. La Salle, Ill.: Open Court, 1985.

Eisendrath-Young, P. *Hags and Heroes*. Toronto: Inner City Books, 1984.

Eliade, M. *Terra Mater and Cosmic Hieros Gamos*. Dallas: Spring Publications, 1955.

———. *The Myth of the Eternal Return*. Princeton: Princeton University Press.

Fallaci, O. *Letter to a Child Never Born*. New York: Simon & Schuster, 1975.

Feher, L. *The Psychology of Birth*. New York: Continuum, 1981.

Fiorenza, E. *In Memory of Her*. New York: Crossroads, 1984.

Firth, R. *Elements of Social Organization,* 3rd ed. London: Tavistock Publications, 1961.

von Franz, M.-L. Archetypes Surounding Death. *Quadrant* 1979:5–23.

———. *Projection and Re-Collection in Jungian Psychology*. La Salle, Ill., and London: Open Court, 1980.

———. *On Dreams and Death*. Boston: Shambhala Books, 1986.

Frazer, J. G. *The Golden Bough: A Study in Magic and Religion*. London: Mac-Millan Press, 1922.

Freud, S. Mourning and Melancholia. In *Freud: General Psychological Theory,* Joseph Strachey, ed. New York: Collier Books, 1963.

Furman, E. P. The Death of a Newborn: Care of the Parents. *Birth Fam. J.* 5 (1978):214–18.

Garfield, C. A. A Child Dies. In *Stress and Survival*, C. A. Garfield, ed. St. Louis: C. V. Mosby Co., 1979.

van Gennep, A. *The Rites of Passage*. Chicago: University of Chicago Press, 1909.

Gorer, G. Death, Grief and Mourning in Britain. In *The Child and His Family: The Impact of Disease and Death*, E. J. Anthony and C. Koupernik, eds. New York: John Wiley, 1973.

Greer, G. *Sex and Destiny*. New York: Harper & Row, 1984.

Grimm, The Brothers. *Fairy Tales: Complete Edition*. London: Routledge & Kegan Paul, 1975.

Hall, N. *The Moon and the Virgin*. New York: Harper & Row, 1980.

Harding, M. E. *The Way of All Women*. New York: G. P. Putnam's Sons, 1970.

———. *Women's Mysteries*. New York: G. P. Putnam's Sons, 1983.

Hillman, J. *In Search: Psychology and Religion*. London and New York: Charles Scribner, 1967.

———. *Loose Ends*. Zurich: Spring Publications, 1975.

———. The Bad Mother: An Archetypal Approach. *Spring* 1983:165–82.

———. *Archetypal Psychology: A Brief Account*. Dallas: Spring Publications, 1983.

Horowitz, M. J. *Stress Response Syndromes*. New York: Jason Aronson, 1976.

Ilse, S. *Empty Arms*. Long Lake, Minn.: Wintergreen Press, 1982.

Jacobi, J. *Complex, Archetype and Symbol in the Psychology of C. G. Jung*. Princeton: Princeton University Press, 1959.

Jacoby, M. *The Way of Individuation*. New York: Harcourt Brace, 1965.

Jameson, A. B. *Legends of the Madonna*. London: Unit Library Ltd., 1904.

Jegen, C. F. *Mary According to Women*. Kansas City: Leaven Press, 1985.

Jimenez, S. *The Other Side of Pregnancy*. Englewood Cliffs, N.J.: Prentice-Hall, 1982.

Jung, C. G. *The Stages of Life: Man in Search of a Soul*. New York: Harcourt Brace, 1939.

———. *Answer to Job*. In *Collected Works*, vol. 11. Princeton: Princeton University Press, 1958, 1969.

———. "The Symbolic Life." Lecture 1939; Guild of Pastoral Psychology No. 38, April 1954.

———. *Symbols of Transformation.* In *Collected Works*, vol. 5. Princeton: Princeton University Press, 1956.

———. *Memories, Dreams, Reflections.* New York: Random House, 1961.

———. *Two Essays on Analytical Psychology.* In *Collected Works*, vol. 7. Princeton: Princeton University Press, 1966.

———. *Aion: Researches into the Phenomenology of the Self.* In *Collected Works*, vol. 9/ii. Princeton: Princeton University Press, 1968a.

———. *Psychology and Alchemy.* In *Collected Works*, vol. 12. Princeton: Princeton University Press, 1968b.

———. *The Structure and Dynamics of the Psyche.* In *Collected Works*, vol. 8. Princeton: Princeton University Press, 1969a.

———. *The Archetypes and the Collective Unconscious.* In *Collected Works*, vol. 9/i. Princeton: Princeton University Press, 1969b.

———. *Psychology and Religion: West and East.* In *Collected Works*, vol. 11. Princeton: Princeton University Press, 1969c.

———. *Psychological Types.* In *Collected Works*, vol. 6. Princeton: Princeton University Press, 1971.

———. *The Symbolic Life.* In *Collected Works*, vol. 18. Princeton: Princeton University Press, 1976.

Kaplan, D. M., and A. Smith *et al.* Family Mediation of Stress. *Social Work* 18 (1973):60–69.

Kaufman, G. *Shame.* Cambridge, Mass.: Schenkonan Pub. Co. Inc., 1980.

Kavanaugh, R. E. *Facing Death.* Baltimore: Penguin Books, 1974.

Kitzinger, S., and J. A. Davis, eds. *The Place of Birth.* New York: Oxford University Press, 1978.

Klaus, M. H., and J. H. Kennell. The Mourning Response of Parents to the Death of a Newborn. *N. Eng. J. Med.* 1970:283.

———. *Parent-Infant Bonding.* St. Louis: C. V. Mosby, 1982.

———. *The Beginnings of Parent-Infant Attachment.* New York: New American Library, 1983.

Knapp, R. J. *Beyond Endurance: When a Child Dies.* New York: Schocken Books, 1986.

Kolbenschlag, Madonna. *Kiss Sleeping Beauty Goodbye.* New York: Bantam Books, 1979.

Kübler-Ross, E. *On Death and Dying.* New York: MacMillan, 1969.

Langer, S. *Philosophy in a New Key.* Cambridge: Harvard University Press, 1942.

Laski, M. *Ecstasy: A Study of Some Secular and Religious Experiences.* Bloomington: Indiana University Press, 1961.

Levine, S. *Meetings at the Edge.* New York: Anchor Press, 1984.

Lewis, E. The Management of Stillbirth: Coping with an Unreality. *Lancet* 2 (1976):619–20.

Lifton, R. J. *The Broken Connection: On Death and the Continuity of Life.* New York: Basic Books, Inc., 1983.

Lindemann, E. Symptomatology and Management of Acute Grief. *American Journal of Psychiatry* 101:141–49.

Loving Arms Newsletter. Wayzata, Minn.: Pregnancy and Infant Loss Center of
   Minnesota.
MacFarlane, J. A., D. M. Smith, & D. H. Garrow. The Relationship Between
   Mother and Neonate. In *The Place of Birth*, S. Kitzinger & J. A. Davis, eds.
   New York: Oxford University Press, 1978.
Machtiger, H. G. Perilous Beginnings: Loss, Abandonment, and Transforma-
   tion. *Chiron: A Review of Jungian Analysis* 1985:101–29.
Mandelbaum, D. Social Use of Funeral Rites. In *The Meaning of Death*, H.
   Feifel, ed. New York: McGraw-Hill, 1959.
Marris, P. Attachment and Society. In *The Place of Attachment in Human Be-
   havior*, C. W. Parkes & J. Stevenson-Hinde, eds. New York: Basic Books,
   Inc. 1982.
McBride, A. B. *The Growth and Development of Mothers.* New York: Harper &
   Row, 1973.
Meier, C. A. *Ancient Incubation and Modern Psychotherapy.* Evanston, Ill.: North-
   western University Press, 1967.
Mitchell, S. *Selected Poetry of Rainer Maria Rilke.* New York: Vintage Books,
   1980.
Mitscherlich, A., and M. Mitscherlich. *The Inability to Mourn.* New York:
   Grove Press.
Mollenkott, V. *The Divine Feminine.* New York: Crossroad, 1984.
Mudd, P. The Fear of Death as a Factor in Individuation. Unpublished thesis,
   1983. Available through C. G. Jung Institute of Chicago, Evanston, Ill.
Neumann, E. *The Great Mother: Analysis of the Archetype.* Princeton: Princeton
   University Press, 1963.
——. *The Origins and History of Consciousness.* Princeton: Princeton Univer-
   sity Press, 1970.
——. The Psychological Meaning of Ritual. *Quadrant* 1976:5–34.
Olsen, C., ed. *The Book of the Goddess.* New York: Crossroads, 1983.
Palinski, C. O., and H. Pizer. *Coping with a Miscarriage.* New York: New
   American Library, 1980.
Panuthos, C., and C. Romeo. *Ended Beginnings: Healing Childbearing Losses.*
   South Hadley, Mass.: Begin & Garvey Pub. Co. Inc., 1984.
Parkes, C. M. The First Year of Bereavement. *Psychiatry* 33 (1970):444–67.
——. Psycho-social Transitions: A Field Study. *Social Science & Medicine* 5
   (1971):101–15.
——. *Bereavement.* New York: International Universities Press, 1972.
——. *The Place of Attachment in Human Behavior.* New York: Basic Books,
   Inc., 1982.
Peppers, L. G., and R. J. Knapp. *Motherhood and Mourning.* New York: Praeger
   Publishers, 1980.
Pizer, H., and C. Palinski. *Coping with a Miscarriage.* Mosby: Plume, 1980.
Portman, A. *New Paths in Biology.* New York: Harper & Row, 1964.
Preston, J., ed. *Mother Worship.* Chapel Hill, N.C.: University of North Caro-
   lina Press, 1982.
Rado, S. The Problem of Melancholia. *International J. of Psychoanalysis* 9 (1928):
   420–38.

Rajadhon, P. A. *Life and Ritual in Old Siam.* New Haven, Conn.: HRAF Press, n.d.

Raphael, B. *The Anatomy of Bereavement.* New York: Basic Books, 1982.

Rhys-Davies, C. *Psalms of the Sisters*: Pali Text Society, *Psalms of the Early Buddhists.* Oxford: Oxford University Press, 1932.

Rich, A. *Of Women Born.* New York: W. W. Norton & Co., 1976.

Rosenblatt, P. C. *Bitter, Bitter Tears.* Minneapolis, Minn.: University of Minnesota Press, 1983.

———, P. Walsh, and D. Jackson. *Grief and Mourning in Cross-Cultural Perspective.* New Haven, Conn.: HRAF Press, 1976.

Ruether, R. R. *Mary: The Feminine Face of the Church.* Philadelphia: Westminster Press, 1977.

Samuels, A. *Jung and the Post-Jungians.* London: Routledge & Kegan Paul, 1985.

———, B. Shorter, and F. Plaut. *A Critical Dictionary of Jungian Analysis.* London and New York: Routledge & Kegan Paul, 1986.

Sanders, N. K., ed. and trans. *Poems of Heaven and Hell from Ancient Mesopotamia.* Middlesex, England: Penguin Books, 1971.

Satinover, J. At the Mercy of Another: Abandonment and Restitution in Psychosis and Psychotic Character. *Chiron: A Review of Jungian Analysis* 1985: 47–86.

Schiff, H. S. *The Bereaved Parent.* New York: Penguin Books, 1978.

Stein, M. *Jung's Treatment of Christianity: The Psychotherapy of a Religious Tradition.* Wilmette, Ill.: Chiron Publications, 1985.

Stevens, A. *Archetypes: A Natural History of the Self.* New York: Quill, 1983.

Stone, M. *Ancient Mirrors of Womanhood.* Boston: Beacon Press, 1979.

Ulanov, A. B. *The Feminine.* Evanston, Ill.: Northwestern University Press, 1971.

de Vries, A. *Dictionary of Symbols and Imagery.* Amsterdam and London: North Holland Pub. Co.

Warner, M. *Alone of All Her Sex: The Myth and Cult of the Virgin Mary.* New York: Alfred A. Knopf, 1976.

Whitmont, E. C. *Return of the Goddess.* New York: Crossroads, 1984.

Wolff, J. R., et al. The Emotional Reaction to a Stillbirth. *Amer. J. Obstet. & Gynaecol*:108 (1970):73–76.

Wolkstein, D. The Dream of Dumuzi. *Quadrant* 1982:55–62.

Woodfield, R. L., and L. L. Viney. Bereavement: A Personal Construct Approach. In press.

Woodman, M. *The Pregnant Virgin: A Process of Psychological Transformation.* Toronto: Inner City Books, 1985.

Index

Sanders, N., 16
Satinover, J., 70
Schiff, H. S., 61–62
Search
  in dreams, 56–58
  as stage of mourning, 49–65
Self, the, 11, 22, 29, 46, 75, 76–77, 87,
  94–95, 101, 108
  child as nonpersonal, 32
  inflation and identification with, 19, 20
Self-sacrifice, 18. *See also* Suicide
Separation process, 7, 17–18. *See also*
  Detachment
Shadow grief, 8, 26–30, 60
Shame, 58–60, 102–103
Shand, A. F., 64
"The Sitting Time" (Digman), 25
Somatic distress, as symptom of grief,
  xiii, 6
"Some People" (Flavia), 79–80
Spirits, reality of, 45–46
Stein, M., 83–84, 102
Stevens, A., 33, 38, 104
"Stillborn" (Clark), 9–10
Stillborn loss, 2, 51. *See also* Perinatal
  death
  and refusal to bear children, 3–4
Stress-response syndrome, 6
Subtle body, concept of, 69, 75–76
Sudden Infant Death Syndrome (SIDS), 2
"Suffering and Incarnation" (Corbett), 11
Suicidal ideation
  as symptom of grief, 6
Suicide, 16, 18, 20, 55, 62, 104
Surviving children
  loss of love for, 12
Symptomatology of grief, 6

Tears, as symbol, 65
"The Tenth Elegy" (Rilke), 79
Terminal illness
  long-term, of child, 4
  five-phase process of mourning in, 6
Thanatological psychology, 6, 29
Therapy
  need to acknowledge childbirth loss in,
    102–103
  termination of, 105–106
"Thoughts on a Fifth Anniversary" (Heil),
  27–28
Tolerance
  increased, 8, 26
Transcendent function, 22–23, 92–93,
  108
Transference/countertransference, 103,
  105
Transformation, 19, 84, 96
  as intended culmination of ritual, 45

Transformative nature of grief, 5, 11, 21,
  84–85
Transpersonal experience, 11, 19
Trauma
  of birthing, 32–33

Unkemptness, as aspect of mourning,
  50, 56

Values, change of, 8, 26
Vow to never forget, 8–15

Waiting, 19
Warner, M., 55, 56, 86
Water, as symbol, 65
Way, the, archetype of, 47, 89
The Way of All Women (Harding), 17
Weeping, 64–65
Whitmont, E. C., 76–77
Wish to die, 8, 15–18
Wolff, J. R., 3
Woodfield and Viney, 29

Yearning, 49–65